MW01505786

REDEEMING THE
GREAT EMANCIPATOR

The Nathan I. Huggins Lectures

REDEEMING

THE

GREAT EMANCIPATOR

Allen C. Guelzo

Harvard University Press

Cambridge, Massachusetts, and London, England

2016

Library of Congress Cataloging-in-Publication Data

Guelzo, Allen C.
    Redeeming the great emancipator / Allen C. Guelzo.
        pages cm. — (The Nathan I. Huggins lectures)
    Includes bibliographical references and index.
    ISBN 978-0-674-28611-5 (cloth : alk. paper)
    1. Lincoln, Abraham, 1809–1865—Views on slavery.   2. Slaves—
Emancipation—United States.   3. United States. President
(1861–1865 : Lincoln). Emancipation Proclamation.   4. Lincoln,
Abraham, 1809–1865—Influence.   I. Title.
    E457.2.G886 2016
    973.7092—dc23   2015017376

For Skip Gates

CONTENTS

PREFACE

THESE LECTURES began their life as the 2012 Nathan I. Huggins Lectures at Harvard University, under the sponsorship of the W. E. B. Du Bois Institute for African and African American Research. There is an appropriateness to this set of circumstances. My first undergraduate research paper was written on Nathan Huggins's history of the Harlem Renaissance; and a portrait of W. E. B. Du Bois hangs in the Civil War Era Studies program office at Gettysburg College. And there are few, if any, pleasanter places in the groves of academe than Harvard, and particularly for me, having spent the 1994–1995 academic year there as a Fellow of the Charles Warren Center for American Studies. It was there that I hatched the first egg of my studies of Abraham Lincoln, a paper entitled "Lincoln and the Doctrine of Necessity," which was subsequently published in the *Journal of the Abraham Lincoln Association* and which became the head from which sprang *Abraham Lincoln: Redeemer President* in 1999. I had not actually come to Harvard to write about Lincoln; I was pursuing a project at the University of Pennsylvania on the history of determinism and free will in American thought. I turned to Lincoln only because I knew that Lincoln had, early in his career as a politician, offered up some surprisingly sophisticated comments on the subject. The kind of book I had in mind at that point could do nothing but benefit from the juice it would enjoy from having Abraham Lincoln make a cameo appearance. But the reception of the article was far more interesting than I could have ever dreamt, and like the child who cannot get his hand out of the cookie jar, I found myself trapped with the guilty goods. I cannot, of course, complain at the result. It was probably a more typical Harvardian turn of events than I would have imagined.

To return to Harvard eighteen years afterward (with a few less demanding visits interspersed) had some of the elements of a reunion. My principal host was Henry Louis Gates Jr., Alphonse Fletcher University Professor at Harvard and the director of the Du Bois Institute, whom I first met, not at Harvard, but in Gettysburg while he was in the midst of filming his Public Broadcasting Service documentary *Looking for Lincoln*. I will acknowledge from the first the peculiar spell Skip Gates can cast, and admit that I can speak of no profounder mutual curiosity and fellowship than the one which we have shared. On the evening that I learned of his absurd arrest for the "crime" of entering his own home, I could think of no better message to send by e-mail than "cuffed to you." I would say it again, and under virtually any other circumstances, too. I thank him in particular for the honor of delivering these lectures, both as a nonresident Fellow of the Du Bois Institute and as a friend.

Harvard also called me back into the fellowship of other friends, old and new. Principal among these is, and will always be, Professor James W. Hankins, founder and general editor of the I Tatti Renaissance Library, whom I have known for nearly all my life. Along with him stand Harvey Mansfield, Harvard's William R. Kenan Jr. Professor of Government; William Julius Wilson, the Lewis P. and Linda L. Geyser University Professor at Harvard and the only sociologist I can honestly say that I have read and understood; and the Reverend Eugene F. Rivers, pastor of the Azusa Christian Community in Dorchester and cofounder of the Boston TenPoint Coalition. I had admired Gene Rivers's work in the Boston area for many years, but from afar, remembering the years I had spent in ministry in west Philadelphia; when Gene introduced himself at the close of the first of these lectures, I almost involuntarily sank down on one knee in tribute. A real drama queen, yes, I know, but the gesture was the face on some long, deep meanings.

The Nathan I. Huggins Lectures take as their subject Abraham Lincoln and emancipation. In practice, however, they use Lincoln's reputation as the "Great Emancipator" as a revelation of markers in cultural maturation, and especially our perceptions of race and responsibility. I have no particular agenda or solution for the ongoing agony of racial inequality to promote. Every such cure I have seen and heard over the decades has usually broken down in one way or another. Moments of optimism that the cloud of racial antagonism is lifting get sharply reined in by unlooked-for interpositions of evil and injustice. I recall all too clearly witnessing, with a sort of sick impotence, a black colleague pulled over by a policeman in the elite white suburb where we then both taught, for no other crime than "d.w.b." (driving while black), and I have had to watch upscale black parents routinely instruct their sons about how to respond to the inevitable police pat-downs as though felony was their default disposition. As I write this preface, yet another shooting of an unarmed black teenager by a policeman in Ferguson, Missouri, has exploded into rioting and racial recrimination.

And yet, the seasons of despair are lightened by shafts of racial goodness and brotherhood. A black pastor in Ferguson, Willis Johnston, restrained an angry African American youth with words which come home like truth: "This is not a race issue, in and of itself. This is a human issue. . . . And if you're honest and you're true, you can't help but look at other people and look at situations and say, 'But by the grace of God go you—and me.'" In west Philly in the years I worked there, the "solutions" being bandied about had no connection to the problems, and people—usually clergy—had to take charge of their own communities or politely beg well-intentioned city and nongovernmental organization officials to shut up and listen to what *they* saw as the problems. Harold Dean Trulear, whom I have known and revered for many years, forced me to understand that the professionalism which human services providers and the criminal justice system bring to bear often weaken rather than strengthen the communities they seek to help. What African Americans want is not white largesse—and the rotted cream of condescension which comes with it—but the productive power to define their own problems and goals; to become citizens, and not clients; friends, not servants.[1] "We are not enemies, but friends," Lincoln said in 1861. Denying that intrinsic relationship as the slaveholders did was what brought us civil war.

Yet, there are interests which are served by dependency, especially when dependency can be masked as service. The trouble is that sicknesses cured by service only make the illness of related sicknesses seem all the more hopeless. As Alexis de Tocqueville observed long ago, the more real equality Americans achieve, the more grating the remaining inequalities feel. "When equality is the common law of a society; the strongest inequalities do not strike the eye; when everything is nearly on a level, the least of them wound it," so that "the desire for equality always becomes more insatiable as equality is greater." Ultimately, I believe that our divisions and inequalities can only find healing—as apart from mere exhausted compromise—in a citizenship that transcends even that of nations and republics, in which (as Lincoln said four years later) the Judge of all the earth does right.

No more of hatred than in Heaven itself,
No more of jealousy than in Paradise.

The importance I attribute to Lincoln is partly a matter of personal professional expertise and interest, but also partly a matter of anxiety that, unless we can understand why Lincoln remains the "Great Emancipator," we will not only lose him but show in a highly dramatic way how we are losing each other. Race in America is a story for whites as well as blacks; Lincoln is a piece of African American history as much as Civil War history; and the fate of African Americans is tied to the fate of all other Americans. Inequality, as William Julius Wilson reminded us, is a problem for black, white, Latinos, and Asians *together,* as Americans, as citizens, as friends.[2] For ultimately, we are indeed all in this *together.*

The Emancipation Proclamation, January 1, 1863.

National Archives

Et miraris quod paucis placeo cui cum paucis convenit, cui omnia fere aliter videntur ac vulgo, a quo semper quod longissime abest id penitus rectum iter censeo.

Are you surprised that there are only a few like me? I don't run with the crowd. I've always thought the right path to be the one as far away from the crowd as possible.

Petrarch, *Epistolae de rebus familiaribus*

1

THE UNWANTING OF
ABRAHAM LINCOLN

EVERY REPUTATION has a shelf life. Abraham
Lincoln thought that the reputation of George Washington was nearly as resistant to decay as any reputation could be: "Washington is the mightiest name of
earth—long since mightiest in the cause of civil liberty; still mightiest in moral reformation," he said in
1842. "To add brightness to the sun, or glory to the
name of Washington, is alike impossible."[1] Or if not
Washington, then certainly the reputation of the
Union soldiers whose cemetery he dedicated at Gettysburg in 1863 was beyond "our poor power to add
or detract." So for Lincoln himself. George Boutwell
(Massachusetts congressman, senator, cabinet secretary, drafter of the Fourteenth Amendment, member
of the Harvard Board of Overseers) claimed for Lincoln "the place next to Washington, whether we have
regard to private character, to intellectual qualities,
to public services, or to the weight of obligation laid

upon the country and upon mankind." Boutwell rested that claim on "three great papers" from Lincoln's hand—"the proclamation of emancipation, his oration at Gettysburg, and his second inaugural address." But especially the Emancipation Proclamation. Lincoln "was personally the enemy of slavery, and he ardently desired its abolition." Emancipation was his path, "and he walked fearlessly in it." The proclamation thus became his passport to immortality. "If all that Lincoln said and was should fail to carry his name and character to future ages, the emancipation of four million human beings by his single official act is a passport to all of immortality that earth can give."[2]

Boutwell was far from the only one of Lincoln's contemporaries to draw this conclusion. "Looking at the history of the world," concluded Edward F. Bullard, "the PROCLAMATION of January 1, 1863, is the greatest event within the last eighteen hundred years." Massachusetts governor John Albion Andrew, who had repeatedly criticized Lincoln's slowness in issuing the proclamation, hailed its appearance in September, 1862, as "a mighty act . . . grand and sublime after all." The abolition journalist Moncure Daniel Conway thought he "had witnessed the final combat between Jesus and Satan in America," that "in the proclamation . . . a victorious sun appeared about to rise upon the New World of free and equal men." The philosopher-general, Ethan Allan Hitchcock, called the proclamation "the most important paper that has emanated from this government since the foundation of the Constitution." And Missouri politician Charles D. Drake, who had been as reluctant for emancipation as John Andrew had been impatient, assured his hearers in January 1863, "My friends, if any words have, in the history of the world, emanated from the ruler of any people, which had a more august and enduring import than those, I know not of them. An involuntary feeling of awe rises within me as I read them, and endeavor to scan their probable influence upon the future of America and of humanity. They ring out the glad peal of this nation's deliverance." Lincoln's vice president, the Maine abolitionist Hannibal Hamlin, wrote Lincoln as soon as the preliminary version of the proclamation was released to say that "it will stand as the great act of the age," and like Boutwell, Hamlin predicted that "future generations will, as I do, say God bless you this great and noble act."[3]

Boutwell, Hamlin, and the others were, as we know, wrong; and so was Lincoln about Washington. We live in a "world come of age," a world in which any and

all questions of significance are answered without
resorting to authority, and in which our lives are
perfectly manageable on a day-to-day basis without
reference to the leading strings of ethics, religion,
law, or history. In such a world, heroic reputations of
the sort Lincoln, Hamlin, and Boutwell described
seem as bizarre as the heroic statuary of Lenin and
Saddam Hussein; only those still in their cultural
adolescence will accept the condescending pennies
of the past for guidance or gift, or even care enough
to make the adolescent's conventional statement of
prematurity, by pulling the statuary down. In a world
come of age, space is won by demonstrations of weakness and suffering, not strength and genius; serious-
ness is mocked as inauthenticity and surface. Dietrich Bonhoeffer, who may be said to have authored the
concept of a world come of age, spoke of how pointless it is in such a world to expect acknowledgments
of intellectual or moral indebtedness: "Pointless, because it seems to me like an attempt to put a grown-up
man back into adolescence, i.e. to make him dependent on things on which he is, in fact, on longer dependent, and thrusting him into problems that are,
in fact, no longer problems for him." There are no
otherworldly qualities which lift individuals above
the flux of human events, and we become radically

suspicious of the present, without illusions but also without hope.[4] This viewpoint has been particularly to the advantage of reductionists who believe that nothing else explains human behavior except the will to power—that literature, music, art, politics, and life are but the disguises and strategies worn by oppressors. These putative oppressors have been as various and numerous as they have been vapid—Jews, kulaks, intellectuals, infidels, Masons, Bilderbergs, Trilaterals, space aliens—but the description of them has in common this single theme, that what we once, in our innocence, mistook *as* innocence is in fact a concatenation of the cunning and disreputable, such as only adults can understand. We are compelled to live, said Bonhoeffer, "in the world *etsi deus non daretur,*" as if God were "weak and powerless in the world." Every foot is clay; every glass seen through darkly. *You got to break your own chains,* we say, *you got to walk that lonesome valley. Nobody here can walk it with you.*

There is a certain congeniality of this discount cynicism to the American grain. John Winthrop stepped off the *Arbella,* fully convinced that everyone had to grapple personally, without the intervention of priest or sacrament, with the demon of total depravity; the Great Awakening demanded absolute and immediate conversion, and the separation of personal experience from a natural law shared with the rest of the world; the singularity of the American founding as a republic in a universe of monarchies made every nonrepublican gesture suspect. Even Lincoln entertained a certain amount of suspicion of heroic biography. "Biographies as written are false and misleading," Lincoln told his law partner William Henry Herndon.

> "The author of the Life of his love paints him as a perfect man, magnifies his perfections and suppresses his imperfections, describes the success of his love in glowing terms, never once hinting at his failures and his blunders. Why do not," said Lincoln, "book merchants and sellers have blank biographies on their shelves always ready for sale, so that, when a man dies, if his heirs, children, and friends wish to perpetuate the memory of the dead, they can purchase one already written, but with blanks, which they can fill up eloquently and grandly at pleasure, thus commemorating a lie, an injury to the dying and to the name of the dead?"[5]

But occasional splashes of suspicion and cynicism are one thing; an entire cultural hermeneutic of suspicion is another, and it is that to which we have come, along with the apprehension that the discovery of woundedness is the modern coming-of-age ritual.

Suspicion should be distinguished from prudence, but making this distinction is not as easy as it sounds. For the twelve million or so blacks torn from their African homelands during the long midnight of the transatlantic slave trade, and their four million descendants who labored without recompense and without hope as slaves in the American republic in 1860, prudence required the deployment of suspicion on a daily, even hourly basis, simply in the interest of survival. That suspicion was directed at white people—not just the whites who, putatively, owned them in the same way they owned cattle and horses, but *all* white people, North or South, blue or gray, American or foreign. A Union officer on Sherman's march through Georgia did not understand why black slaves did not turn out enthusiastically to greet their liberators. Because, explained one elderly Georgia slave, someone might be taking notes. It was all well and good that the Union armies had come all this way to defeat Johnny Reb, "But, massa, you'se'll go way to-morrow, and anudder white man'll come." The officer could only nod in agreement: "He had never known anything but persecutions and injury from the white man," and he saw no reason "to put faith in any white man." The "Gideonite" white missionaries who descended on the occupied Port Royal Sound (South Carolina) to educate and uplift the freedpeople discovered that "nothing is more evident to those who actually know the Colored, than that while they respect, value, and revere, the good, they want little companionship with the whites." They might "honor and reverence" the idealistic Gideonites as well meaning and well intentioned, "still, when all is done, they fall into their own circle of color for companionship." In Savannah, freedpeople trusted only "people of their own color, and believe that the [white officers] who have addressed them are rebels in disguise." In Fayetteville, "they prayed about as hard for Sherman to go as they had prayed for him to come," since hardly an African American house in the town escaped looting by Sherman's men. The experience "produced this good effect on the minds of the Fayetteville negroes—they no longer believed that every man of Northern birth was necessarily their friend, and they more clearly saw the need of looking to themselves for their own elevation."[6]

Sometimes, suspicion was mistaken for apathy by whites who had difficulty reading the contours of

black community. "It was thought at the commence-
ment of the work" of recruiting black Union soldiers
that "a brigade would be formed by this time," complained the *Washington National Intelligencer* in June
1863. But despite "a colored population of six or seven
thousand men" in the contraband camps around the
capital, "enlistments are few," and the first conclusion
was that blacks "seem perfectly willing that the 'white
folks' may do every thing for them"—that is, until it
occurred to the *Intelligencer* that the real problem was
the "jealousy existing between the resident free colored people" of the District of Columbia "and the
contrabands," the former expecting to receive com-
missions to command the latter, and the latter not
particularly wanting such officers. And white Northerners who expected to be hailed by African Americans with thankful cringes sometimes got a rude
awakening: "They are," wrote one astonished white
soldier in the 46th New York, the "most impudent
Set that I have ever seen. When they meet a Yankee on
the street they will hoop at you and hollow, 'Their
goes one of Lincolns hirelings he gets his hard
crackers, Salt horse and $13 per Month.' This is the
thanks we get from the black rascals. . . . They would
cut the throats of Every Yankee for five cents per
head." When a desperate Confederate Congress, in

the Confederacy's last weeks of life, voted to autho-
rize the recruitment of black soldiers with the lure
of emancipation as the reward, there were actually
black volunteers. Not out of love, loyalty, or fidelity
to the old massa, or with the straw hat held subser-
viently in the hand, but out of frank, unadulterated
calculation. "Freedom and liberty is the word with
the Collered people," wrote a free black Louisianan;
if fighting for the Confederacy "makes us free we are
happy to hear it."[7] All white promises were equally
*in*credible, and therefore equally credible, to be picked
up and used as seemed most opportune.

Yet, as much as black prudence justified black suspicion, what is noticeable in these encounters is the
relief with which suspicion could also be laid by, and
especially in the case of Abraham Lincoln. Frederick
Douglass greeted Lincoln's inauguration in 1861 with
something much less than enthusiasm: "Mr. Lincoln
opens his address by announcing his complete loyalty
to slavery in the slave States . . . and how he regards
the right to recapture fugitive slaves a constitutional
duty." He snarled at Lincoln's speech in August 1862,
to "a committee of colored men," asking them to
support colonization: "In this address Mr. Lincoln
assumes the language and arguments of an itin-
erant Colonization lecturer, showing all his incon-

sistencies, his pride of race and blood, his contempt for Negroes and his canting hypocrisy." But Douglass was writing as a *provocateur,* reaching for hyperbole as the lever to move the indifferent into action. His actual encounters with Lincoln, beginning in the summer of 1863, had quite a different effect on him. John Eaton met Douglass at the home of "a wealthy colored man in the city" of Washington, where he found Douglass

> pacing the long, old-fashioned parlors in a state of extreme agitation. "I have just come from President Lincoln," he said, making no attempt to suppress his excitement. "He treated me as a man; he did not let me feel for a moment that there was a difference in the color of our skins! The President is a most remarkable man. I am satisfied now that he is doing all that circumstances will permit him to do. He asked me a number of questions, which I am preparing to answer in writing," and he pointed to the writing materials on a table near him.

In the end, Douglass conceded that Lincoln was "the one man of all the millions of our countrymen to whom we are more indebted for a United Nation and for American liberty than to any other."[8]

Douglass was not the only one. John McCline, a Louisiana slave, recalled that in 1860, "there was much excitement and political talk" among his fellow slaves "over the possible election of Abraham Lincoln as President of the United States." Apart from the unnoticed tribute this paid to the slaves' grape-vine telegraph, even as far away as the sugar-cane fields, what was peculiar was the automatic assumption that "if Lincoln was elected . . . he was against slavery and would use every means in his power to crush it." Slaves in Beaufort, South Carolina, invented stories about Lincoln visiting "Beaufort befo' de war and et dinner to Col. Paul Hamilton" and "left his gold-headed walking cane deer and ain't nobody know de president of de United States been to Beaufort 'till he write back and tell um to look behind de door and send um his gold-headed walking cane. . . ." In another version, Lincoln "come to Beaufort 'fore de war . . . as uh rail-splitter and spy 'round." Charity Austin claimed to have seen Lincoln in disguise before the war, spying on Georgia's slaveholders.

> Abraham Lincoln come through once, but none of us knew who he was. He wus just the raggedest man you ever saw. The white children and me saw him out at the railroad. We were

sittin' and waitin' to see him. He said he wus
huntin' his people; and dat he had lost all he
had. Dey give him somethin' to eat and tobacco
to chew and he went on. Soon we heard he wus
in de White House then we knew who it wus
come through. We knowed den it wus Abraham
Lincoln.[9]

One of the blue-blood Gideonites at Port Royal was
puzzled to find that "it was with difficulty some could
be made to believe he was not a Colored man, who
went around, begging for jobs of rails to split, till he
was made president." Other stories had Lincoln
leading black Union soldiers onto plantations and
freeing the slaves personally, telling them, "You ain't
got no more master and no more missus" and opening
the plantation smokehouse to tell the newly emancipated slaves, "Help yourselves; take what you need;
cook yourselves a good meal!" In the fall of 1862, when
Lincoln visited Frederick, Maryland, "a large crowd
of colored people . . . cheered and kept on cheering
until he was compelled to come out and respond in a
little speech from the door step, and a wonderfully
strong, brave and hopeful speech it was, too." And
when Lincoln issued the final version of the Emancipation Proclamation on January 1, 1863, they

took him at his word: forty-two of the one hundred slaves on Anthony Zimmel's Lingamore plantation, near Frederick, ran off that day, even though the proclamation did not actually include them. The proclamation, wrote William Henry Singleton in his memoir of slavery, "made me and all the rest of my race free. We could not be bought and sold any more or whipped or made to work without pay." Black soldiers at Port Hudson unanimously adopted a Christmas resolution that year, describing "our love for the President of the United States. . . . Language is too weak to convey that estimation in which we hold him." Six months later, a brigade of black troops in Virginia greeted Lincoln with shouts of "Hurrah for the Liberator, Hurrah for the President." In liberated Richmond, "the colored population was wild enthusiasm" when they saw Lincoln walk the streets of the captured Confederate capital. "Old men thanked God in a very boisterous manner, and old women shouted upon the pavement as high as they had ever done at a religious revival" because "when they saw Abraham Lincoln they were satisfied that their freedom was perpetual." In January 1864, more than a year before Frederick Douglass described crashing the Second Inaugural party at Lincoln's invitation, African Americans of "genteel exterior and

the manners of gentlemen" were attending public re-
ceptions at the White House, and at the 1865 New
Year's reception, the newspapers described a "throng"
of black men and women in attendance.[10]

Lincoln's death only triggered more testimonies to
the "great Emancipator." The news of Lincoln's murder
"was so terrible that at first it stunned sensibility. . . .
Men were bereaved, and walked for days as if a corpse
lay unburied in their dwellings." In Port Royal, "the
colored people express their sorrow and sense of
loss in many cases, with sobs and loud lamentations,"
and some feared that they were "going to be slaves
again." On Easter Sunday following the murder, Jacob
Thomas, the pastor of the African Methodist Episcopal Zion Church of Troy, New York, insisted, "We,
as a people, feel more than all others that we are
bereaved."

> We had learned to love Mr. Lincoln as we have
> never loved man before. We idolized his very
> name. We looked up to him as our savior, our
> deliverer. His name was familiar with our
> children, and our prayers ascended to God in
> his behalf. He taught us how to love him. The
> interest he manifested in behalf of the op-
> pressed, the weak and those who had none to

"Freedom to the Slaves," a Currier & Ives print celebrating the Emancipation Proclamation. Although the bending slave kisses Lincoln's hand as the source of his freedom, Lincoln instead points heavenward to redirect attention to freedom's divine origins.

Library of Congress

help them, and won for him a large place in our
heart. It was something so new to us to see such
sentiments manifested by the chief magistrate
of the United States that we could not help but
love him.

Lincoln was "our best friend and warmest advocate,"
preached George L. Ruffin at a "meeting of the colored
people of Richmond" on Easter Monday, April 18,
1865. Lincoln was "the dearest friend, the kindest
man" that "as President" the freed slaves "ever knew,"
declared Henry Highland Garnet during a fund-
raising event for the Thomas Ball Emancipation
statue on July 4, 1865. And it is difficult to dismiss
this praise as only calculated utterances, designed to
ensure the standing of the speakers in the eyes of
whites. "Our Moses had been slain," mourned Elijah
Marrs, "and we knew not what the future had in store
for us." He "was indeed our Moses," wrote Alexander
Heritage Newton in his autobiography of slavery and
Civil War soldier service, "He led us forth. He gave us
our freedom."[11]

In fact, for another generation, Lincoln continued
to be the African Americans' "deliverer." "The mightiest draughts from Lethe's stream could not blot him

from the remembrance of the race," insisted William Sanders Scarborough, president of Wilberforce University, in 1899, for Lincoln was "that second Abraham who, true to his name as the 'father of the faithful,' struck the chains from the Negro's limbs and bade him stand forever free." James Weldon Johnson's *Lift Every Voice and Sing,* the unofficial African American national anthem, was written to be recited "by school children—a chorus of five hundred voices" at a Lincoln's birthday celebration in Jacksonville, Florida, in 1900. AME Zion bishop Alexander Walters, addressing a throng at Carnegie Hall on the centennial of Lincoln's birth, hailed Lincoln as a "savior, which he proved to be by emancipating 4,000,000. . . . and he will be held in loving remembrance by Afro-Americans as long as the world shall stand." A year later, on the fiftieth anniversary of the proclamation, Albert E. Pillsbury (president of Howard University) lauded the proclamation as "the supreme act" of Lincoln's life, and discerned "the hand of God . . . in it and the man divinely appointed to the work."[12]

Even from the point of view of white people, Lincoln had achieved a tectonic shift in the history of American race. "Prejudice against color is fast going away," wrote a soldier in the 127th Illinois in 1865. "The negroes" are "anxious to read and write, provide themselves, and show themselves men." John W. Forney, the clerk of the Senate, invited people to "look down from the galleries of the two houses . . . you will see . . . Colored Men in Congress, colored men before the highest judicial tribunal, also colored men in the local courts deliberate and practice without insult or interruption. . . . How wonderful is the decay of prejudices that seemed to be eternal!" Wonderful enough, at least, that Alexander Newton believed that not only Lincoln but the entire white North had laid the freedpeople in their debt. "The price of human liberty can never be estimated," Newton wrote in 1910.

> This is especially true of those who knew
> what slavery meant. And the Colored race has
> an endless debt to pay their White friends who
> bought their liberty with their own blood.
> While it is true that the White people brought
> our forefathers here and sold them into
> slavery, which of course they had no right to
> do, this does not diminish the price which the
> same race had to pay to buy us out of the
> slavery into which they had sold us. And it does
> not in the least diminish the debt of gratitude
> which we shall owe them as long as time
> exists.[13]

Actually, it did, despite the almost-palpable sense that the end of the Civil War would usher in, not just emancipation, but an entirely new adjustment in the American habits of race. There is what Randall Kennedy has called a "breadth, depth, and subtlety" in America's "racial divisions," which lulls us into a self-congratulatory satisfaction until the outbreak of some fresh hell reminds us how little those satisfactions may be justified.[14] Side by side with Forney's celebration of African Americans in the public square, the bitterly conservative New York Democratic monthly, the *Old Guard,* remained aghast that Lincoln's administration should "attempt to reconstruct society in the South, and force eight millions of white people to live on equal terms with four millions of negroes." The Lincolnites

> assume not that the condition of the negro
> should be improved, or anything of that kind,
> but that it should be abolished, obliterated,
> stricken out of existence, and that of the white
> man forced on him. Or, in other words, that
> the distinctions of race should be ignored,
> trampled down, disregarded, and whites and
> negroes forced to live together under the same

conditions, or, as they express it, in "impartial freedom" together.[15]

But that seemed to be exactly the course being steered in the last year of the war. Lois Bryan Adams wrote from her perch in Washington that in the Capitol, where "not very long since, it would have been as much as an anti-slavery man's life was worth if he dared to express his sentiments openly," now it was "almost impossible . . . to keep the galleries quiet when a senator or member advocates the constitutional doctrine that 'All men are born free and equal'; there is an involuntary lifting of hands and a thrill of approval felt and seen as if applause were hard to restrain." On the Fourth of July 1863, Adams beheld more wonders: that the "Colored Sabbath Schools and their friends" enjoyed "a splendid picnic in the beautiful shaded park between the President's house and the War Department." It was as though racial differences had vanished:

> It was really a sight world going miles to see.
> There were several thousands of both sexes and
> of all shades and ages decked out in a brilliancy
> of coloring, dazzling to behold. A fine brass
> band of colored musicians, discoursed sweet

music in one part of the grounds; there were
groups of sable singers in another, tables loaded
with refreshments were spread promiscuously
under the trees, and general joy and gladness
seemed to prevail.

And by February 1865, Adams saw what she described,
Galileo-like, as proof "the world moves"—Henry
Highland Garnet "preaching against slavery from
the Speaker's desk in the House of Representatives . . .
and accepted as quietly almost as any ordinary
event."[16]

It seemed almost possible that race itself would dis-
appear as a category. Phillips Brooks, the eloquent
rector of Holy Trinity, Rittenhouse Square, in Philadelphia, thought that the Emancipation Proclamation's dispelling of the cloud of slavery was like
"when a man comes out of a fever" and temporarily
suffers "blindness or deafness." It was time to seize
the moment and push through from emancipation to
full racial egalitarianism. "If the negro is a man, and
we have freed him in virtue of his manhood," asked
Brooks, "what consistency or honor is it which still
objects to his riding down the street in the same cars
with us if he is tired, or sitting in the same pew with
us if he wants to worship God?" And that, argued

Theodore Tilton of the *New York Independent,* should be only the beginning. To turn the slave into a man, and "the man, a citizen; the citizen, a voter!" was only the beginning, "the letter A in the alphabet of Democracy." If the "whole human race are one family,"

"Uncle Sam's Thanksgiving Dinner," a cartoon by Thomas Nast, which appeared in the November 20, 1869, issue of *Harper's Weekly,* enthusiastically celebrates the subordination of race and ethnicity to citizenship in the American Republic, especially with the passage of the Reconstruction amendments to the Constitution. Portraits of Lincoln, Washington, and Ulysses Grant fill the wall, while Uncle Sam carves the turkey for a tableful of races and nationalities. The print behind him shows Castle Garden, which was then New York's processing station for immigrants, and the centerpiece is built on "Self-Government" and "Universal Suffrage."

Tilton concluded, then "we will have no permanent settlement of the negro question till our haughtier white blood, looking the negro in the face, shall forget that he is black, and remember only that he is a citizen." After all, Tilton reasoned, blackness was merely color, and color was far from being a biological absolute. "Already three-fourths of the colored people of the United States have white blood in their veins" through the much dreaded 'miscegenation' and 'amalgamation' that slaveholders simultaneously denounced loudly on platforms but practiced secretly in the quarters. Was it not common knowledge, asked Joel Prentiss Bishop, that black Americans "bear the best and purest white-gentleman blood of the country in their veins, and these were all born of just the mothers whom, in preference to all others, the white-gentleman fathers selected"? And "this intermingling will continue," Tilton prophesied, until "the negro of the South, growing paler with every generation, will at last completely hide his face under the snow." William Lloyd Garrison also wondered whether "as civilization and knowledge, and republican feelings, and Christianity prevail in the world, the wider will matrimonial connexions extend; and finally people of every tribe and kindred and tongue will freely intermarry." It was, perhaps, a predictable conceit on the part of white New Yorkers and Bostonians that blacks should become white rather than whites black, but it was leagues removed from the arrant nonsense being spluttered fruitlessly across town by the *Old Guard,* that "it is an infidel, murderous revolution" to make "negroes what neither God nor the Constitution ever designed they should be, the equal of the white race."[17]

But on Tilton's logic, what sense could racial discrimination make any longer? A year before, Thaddeus Stevens had asked aloud "whether the soldiers of the United States"—and he meant *black* soldiers—"who wear the livery of the Union . . . shall be placed on an equality, or whether in that position . . . we are to keep up the distinctions which have been the infamy, and disgrace of the Union and the age." Not if he could help it. Stevens hoped that "a military tribunal" could be formed "to follow the army" and hold drum-head sales "to the highest bidder" of "the lands of every rebel," with the highest bidder being "military occupants, who with arms in their hands, shall take resident possession . . . and be ready to defend it against all comers." Over the course of that year, Charles Sumner exulted, the Fugitive Slave Law was repealed, the "exclusion of colored persons" on "any of the three rail-roads in the District" had been prohibited, the coastal slave trade (the last remnant of the Atlantic slave trade) was banned, and the "exclusion of colored testimony in U.S. courts prohibited." On January 31, 1865, George Julian of Indiana witnessed the passage of the Thirteenth Amendment by the House of Representatives, and it made him think that he "had been born into a new life, and that the world was overflowing with beauty and joy, while I was inexpressibly thankful for the privilege of recording my name on so glorious a page of the nation's history, and in testimony of an event so long only dreamed of as possible in the distant future." The next day, February 1, John S. Rock was presented by Sumner to plead before the bar of the U.S. Supreme Court, the first African American to be admitted as counsel before a court which a decade before had declared that he was not even a citizen. THE DRED SCOTT DECISION BURIED IN THE SUPREME COURT ran the *New York Tribune*'s headline, "Senator Charles Sumner and the Negro lawyer John S. Rock [were] the pall-bearers—the room of the Supreme Court of the United States the Potter's Field—the corpse the Dred Scott decision!" In Washington, any walker along the streets had to be amazed that "rich and poor, young and old, foul with rags, and decked with gold, the nabob and his dusky brother, once a slave, now pass each other on the freeman's level and all together conspire to make lively times in Washington." Two weeks after Maryland officially abolished slavery, Frederick Douglass returned to Baltimore for the first time since his flight from slavery, twenty-six years before. He was "awed into silence" by the changes which the war had wrought, and as he spoke to a racially mixed meeting at an African American church, he declared that "the revolution is genuine, full and complete." In Mobile, Lawrence S. Berry, a freed slave-turned-journalist, urged his readers to "forget our sable complexion" and close ranks with progressive whites. The faster "we cease to meet as a class in conventions, the better it will be for us as a race." Was it possible that "the white and colored people of this country" could be "blended into a common nationality, and enjoy together in the same country, under the same flag, the inestimable blessings of life, liberty, and the pursuit of happiness, as neighborly citizens of a common country?" asked Douglass. "I answer most unhesitatingly, I believe they can."[18]

Douglass, however, could not have been more wrong, nor the *Old Guard* more right. The revolution was not only *not* complete, but in some places, had never even begun. In 1863, Julian Sturtevant, the

New England–born president of Illinois College, acknowledged that the logic of "emancipation would carry with it the equality of the negro and the white man in all their relations." But logic would have a hard time making way against the "unconquerable aversion" felt toward any plan to "incorporate the negro into the mass of American society." Sturtevant took it for granted that emancipation made no sense unless it would also "admit the negro . . . to all the privileges and franchises of the Constitution, and amalgamate him entirely with the mass of American society." But sense did not always have the upper hand in discussions of race: "such a solution of the question," Sturtevant sadly admitted, is resisted by whites "by a sort of instinct, rather than from set conviction and purpose." Even Thaddeus Stevens privately doubted "whether we shall find any body with a sufficient grasp of mind, and sufficient moral courage, to treat this as a radical revolution, and re-model our institutions." Republicans, insisted Stevens in 1864, "never held such doctrines, never uttered such a wish" for the "amalgamation of the races and to create negro equality." The age of emancipation, rooted in the eighteenth-century Enlightenment, was also the age of scientific racism, and rooted in the racism, racial hierarchy-building, and mystical imputations of identity based on blood, ethnicity, and language formulated by the Romantics. Race, wrote Arthur de Gobineau in his *Essai sur l'inequalite des raises humaines* (1853–1855), was "the master key to the enigma" of history, and throughout the nineteenth century, race became a way of marking biologically fixed cultural characteristics and homogeneous "pure" physical types that would create impenetrable walls of distinction and identity. The German-Swiss zoologist and Darwinist Karl Christoph Vogt, in his 1863 *Lectures on Man: His Place in Creation, and in the History of the Earth* (published by James Hunt in English in 1864 and dedicated to the celebrated Paul Broca), proposed that these racial differences required different designations as species. "Select," Vogt suggested, "the Negro and the German"; then, select "two species of apes which are closely allied, belonging to the same genus and only separated by some slight variations."

> We should not be surprised if you find greater
> differences between Negro and German than
> between the two apes. . . . Species is species, and
> there is but one zoological science, the principles of which must apply equally to man and
> ape, and what in one of these types is called

species must not in the other be called race or variety. If, then, the differences between Negro and German should be greater than those between the capuchin ape, the cebus apellot or the sajou, it would follow that either the two human types must, like those of apes, belong to two different species, or the two acknowledged different species of apes must only form one species. . . . The grown-up Negro partakes, as regards his intellectual faculties, of the nature of the child, the female, and the senile White. He manifests a propensity to pleasure, music, dancing, physical enjoyments, and imitation, while his inconstancy of impressions and all the feelings are those of the child. Like the child, the Negro has no soaring imagination, but he peoples surrounding nature, and endows even lifeless things with human or supernatural powers. He makes himself a Fetish of a piece of wood, and believes that the ape remains dumb lest he should be compelled to work.

Vogt's editor, Hunt, used the platform of the London Anthropological Society and the British Association for the Advancement of Science to deny the existence of any "permanent hybrid Euro-African race," and though Hunt was at pains to "express a hope that the objects of this Society will never be prostituted to such an object as the support of the slave-trade, with all its abuses," nevertheless it remained "the duty of conscientious anatomists carefully to record all deviations from the human standard of organization and analogy with inferior types, which are frequently manifested in the negro race." And so began the long slide backwards, from the unity of the human species to the unchallenged superiority of the white race. "The hue of a negro's skin is in no way an accident," confidently remarked a West Coast editor who, it is probably safe to surmise, had never interacted with African Americans in his life. "The black complexion in the Divine economy, is but the exterior badge of an inferior, coarse human nature, physical and intellectual. To the African, of the negro type, was assigned—not accidentally, but as a part of the All-wise order of the creation—a black skin, of coarse thick texture, crisp, wooly hair surmounting a head and brain altogether distinct in all its characteristics from those of the white man." And alongside the triumph of a racist ideology came a recession from the high-water mark of emancipation and abolition into the collapse of political power in the South back into the hands of the ex-Confederates who had once used that power to attempt the creation of a slave republic; and after that, the even deeper slide into Jim Crow and the political, social, and economic reduction of Southern blacks to peonage and Northern blacks into the ghetto. "Yes, sir," remarked one elderly ex-slave interview by the Works Progress Administration in the 1930s, "they soon found out dat freedom ain't nothin', 'less you got somethin' to live on and a place to call home ... regardless of liberty, love, and all them things."[19]

In casting around for the causes of this failure, it has become conventional to exhume yet another Calvinistic trope, and that is *declension:* white Northerners, forgetting their wartime conversion to racial equality, unity, and solidarity, decided that being white conferred on them a different status, if not a different species identity; and also gave them greater common interests with the defeated Confederates than with their *quondam* black allies—and in a shocking act of betrayal, rewrote their memories of the war to minimize emancipation and maximize sectional reconciliation. The price exacted by the ex-Confederates for this reconciliation was a blind eye for the disenfranchisement and humiliation of black Americans; only blacks themselves retained any memory of a war caused by slavery and fought for emancipation.[20]

This summary has the appeal that all simplifications have; but like all simplifications, it lacks the texture of reality.

There are four causes which lie at the root of the failure of emancipation—if, remembering that "breadth, depth and subtlety" can operate in many ways, *failure* really is the word we should be using. One is a matter of simple politics. Abraham Lincoln was murdered one week after the surrender of the principal Confederate field army at Appomattox, and into his place stepped his ill-chosen vice president, Andrew Johnson. The Indiana Radical Republican, George Julian, "had become intimately acquainted with him while we were fellow members of the Committee on the Conduct of the War," and it made Julian jumpy even then that Johnson "always scouted the idea that slavery was the cause of our trouble, or that emancipation could ever be tolerated without immediate colonization." Although Johnson at first promised to crush the head of the Confederates, he was actually concerned more with the casting down of the white planter elite of the South and its replacement with yeoman Southern whites like himself, rather than the sponsorship of a new black political class. "Damn the Negroes," Johnson told one Tennessee correspondent, "I am fighting these traitorous aristocrats, their masters," and even Johnson's private secretary, William G. Moore, admitted that Johnson "exhibited a morbid distress and feeling against the negroes." With Congress out of session at the time of Lincoln's death, Johnson had a free constitutional hand with which to dispense pardons to deserving Confederates—some 13,000 of them—which not only restored the usual civil rights to vote and to serve in civil offices, but also to acquire business licenses, to sue in civil courts, and above all, to resume title to the lands they had abandoned to their one-time slaves. "The abandoned lands are fast passing back into the hands of their former owners," complained a Freedmen's Bureau worker at Fortress Monroe, and they "are not disposed to help their former slaves to take care of themselves. It is a mystery to me how they live at all. Every day makes their prospects worse. Here and there one makes a little money, but a large majority suffer, and must suffer. I go about emptyhanded, with only words of counsel and sympathy, till I am sick at heart, and each night

I return weary from my five or six miles walk feeling that I have accomplished nothing." Worse than "emptyhanded," Johnson did nothing to prevent Mississippi, Alabama, and South Carolina from adopting "black codes" that spelled slavery in everything but name. "In not a single state has adequate provision been made for the protection of the blacks by civil courts," complained William Grosvenor (economist, journalist, and economic editor of the *New York Tribune*, 1875-1900). There were, conceded the head of the Freedmen's Bureau, Oliver Otis Howard, a class of ex-Confederates who could be "met half way" and who deserved "immunity and pardon." But by and large, Howard found the former Confederates conspiring "openly & secretly to keep the negro in practical slavery." And as soon as "they found that the control of everything was to be again put in their hands," wrote one frantic observer to Radical Republican senator Lyman Trumbull, "they became insolent . . . drunk with power, ruling and abusing every loyal man, white and black."[21]

Congress at once reached to take back the oversight of Reconstruction from Johnson, through the Fourteenth and Fifteenth Amendments to the Constitution, and the First and Second Reconstruction Acts. But long before that time—even before the end of 1865—all the wrong signals had been sent. As the Confederacy's one-time treasury secretary, Christopher Memminger, explained, Johnson "held up before us the hope of a 'white man's government,' and this led us to set aside negro suffrage. . . . It was natural that we should yield to our old prejudices." A slave owner could even hope that, as late as May 1865, emancipation was still a question open to negotiation, or at least, if it "will be the settled policy," Congress would still reserve judgment whether it would be "immediate or gradual" and thus avoid "the shock to the industrial resources of the country."[22]

Veteran Radical Republicans in Congress roared their outrage at Johnson's treachery. George Boutwell covered Johnson with infamy by claiming that "there are three passions to which public men are especially exposed,—fear, hatred, and ambition. Mr. Johnson is the victim and slave of all three," and has "no sympathy with the opinion that the negro is a man and ought to be a citizen." Frederick Douglass was even harsher: Johnson was "ambitious, unscrupulous, energetic, indefatigable, voluble, and plausible . . . a convicted usurper, a political criminal, guilty of a bold and persistent attempt to possess himself of the legislative powers solemnly secured to Congress by the Constitution." The Radicals engineered

Johnson's neutralization, then his impeachment, and finally his excommunication from the ranks of anything that could be considered Republicanism, hailing the election of wartime hero and general Ulysses Grant as president in 1868. Grant turned out to be far friendlier to African American equality than might have been expected, but he was also far less a leader and manager than Lincoln. He was also far too late. By the fall of 1865, William Grosvenor could already see that, even when "slavery is abolished," it was going to be replaced by "peonage, or some other plan of forced labor, hardly less unjust or dangerous to the nation than slavery itself." Still, Radical Republicans and their African American allies might have been able to recover from the Johnson debacle, had it not been for two irreversible facts: one was that the Radical leadership simply began dying off (Thaddeus Stevens in 1868, Salmon Chase in 1873, Charles Sumner in 1874, Henry Wilson in 1875); the other was that it lost elections ("Bluff Ben" Wade, the president *pro tem* of the Senate, was dumped from office in 1869 when his home state legislature was captured by Democrats).[23]

Politics, as much as crackpot racism, was the Achilles' heel of the postwar Reconstruction. The Republicans who carried the Thirteenth Amendment to its successful conclusion in 1865 did so only because the single most solidly anti-Republican bloc of votes—the Democratic South—had subtracted itself; even then, Republicans held onto control in Congress

"The Two Platforms," a campaign poster for Hiester Clymer, the Democratic candidate for governor of Pennsylvania in 1866, appealing to white racial hatred against the Republican candidate, former Union Army Major General John White Geary, whose platform endorsed voting rights for blacks in Pennsylvania and support for the Fifteenth Amendment. The poster also attacks Thaddeus Stevens, John W. Forney, and Simon Cameron. Geary defeated Clymer in the fall 1866 elections.

Library of Congress

more through an appeal to winning the war than to abolishing slavery. Northern Democrats might have been cast into a minority by the departure of their Southern comrades, but they had still garnered 30 percent of the vote in 1860, and garnered still more in the off-year congressional elections in 1862. Had the South not broken away in the winter and spring of 1860–1861, Democrats would have outnumbered Republicans 129 to 108 in the House, and 37 to 29 in the Senate. And much as it is true that Lincoln won an overwhelming reelection in 1864, much of the vote (like the soldier vote, for example) was more anti-Copperhead than Republican. "The holders of slaves," declared Clement Laird Vallandigham, were "nearly always on the side of the Democratic party" and were "the natural ally of the Democracy of the North, and especially of the West." That alliance would soon find ways after the war to repair itself. So, because emancipation was acquiesced-in much more than embraced, many vulnerable Republicans cautiously hedged their political bets: "How can the nation be one again, with such a barrier as those millions of blacks between the two sections, with the apparent antagonism of emancipation on one side and perpetual slavery on the other?" asked Samuel Osgood in March 1865. Promptly, Osgood dodged:

"Precisely what is to be done with the negro we do not profess to say," even though he gingerly inserted the qualifier that "he is a human creature, and ought at once to have the rights of person, property and family that civilization, even in despotic countries, secures to the humblest peasantry."[24]

Democrats were less uncertain. "The man who,—knowing the situation and ignorance of the African race in our country,—favors the extension of the privileges of citizenship to them, is surely reckless of consequences," warned the *Washington Democrat* a week after Lincoln's Second Inaugural. "The ignorance that now exists in the foreign and native born citizens of the United States" was bad enough; the "clamor for negro suffrage" would "launch upon the States a million of black voters, and the consequences are not to be conceived."

> The negroes as a class, possess no capacity for
> self-government, and the few who are intelli-
> gent enough to take part in public affairs are
> offset by the multitude who do not. There
> again this nation of the white race should well
> ponder the question before it admits the African,
> the Mongolian and the Indian races to all its
> privileges. We can be just to them without that,

and the moment the negro becomes a citizen,
the foreign born citizens will be found arrayed
on one side and the negro upon the other, and
the political combinations would assume an
irrepressible antagonism, founded not upon
principles, but upon races. The spirit that John
Brown evoked should not be permitted to
survive this war.

Alongside abolition of slavery, the New Jersey General
Assembly proposed to ban racial intermarriage by
law; California segregated its schools; and although
700,000 new black voters were created in the Reconstruction states, no black voters were created in Wis-
consin, Michigan, Illinois, Missouri, Pennsylvania,
New Jersey, Delaware, Maryland, West Virginia, or
even Connecticut. This left Democrats in Pennsylvania free to campaign in October 1865 under the
banner of promoting "a white man's country," and in
the state elections that fall, they reminded voters
in Philadelphia that "every Republican senator and
representative in Harrisburg now before you for re-
election . . . voted to compel you, your wives and children to ride in cars with Negroes." Democrats ran
an exuberantly racist campaign for the presidency
against Ulysses Grant in 1868, with vice presidential

candidate Francis P. Blair warning luridly that a
"semi-barbarous race" would like nothing more than
to "subject White women to their Unbridled lust."[25]
As it was, Republicans feared that Democratic vic-
tories in the 1866 congressional elections could
embolden Northern and Southern Democrats to
reestablish their old linkage and stage a counter-
Congress protest, and in 1868, only newly enfran-
chised Southern black voters kept Horatio Seymour
from recapturing the presidency for Democrats. An
electorate which had never been more than half
committed to abolition was likely to fall away from
Lincolnian principles once the pressure of the war
was over, and the wonder lies only in the amount of
time it actually took to happen. In the wake of the
panic of 1873, voters handed control of the House of
Representatives to Democrats in 1874, and control of
the Senate in 1878, followed by a Democratic president for the first time since the Civil War in 1884.[26]

Alongside politics sat another factor over which the
Republicans turned out to have little control, and
that was the federal judiciary. The experience of the
Warren Court accustomed us to thinking of the federal courts, rather than national legislation, as the
most effective hammer for breaking down the walls
of discrimination; but this approach to reform was

not feasible in the nineteenth century, and especially not so in the postwar years, when the basest stab at black equality came through the series of U.S. Supreme Court decisions which began with *Slaughterhouse Cases* in 1873, and continued through *United States v. Cruikshank* in 1875, *Civil Rights Cases* in 1883, and finally *Plessy v. Ferguson* in 1896. The drama of the war years has obscured the very real struggle which had been waged since the days of John Marshall and Thomas Jefferson between the branches of the federal government, each jockeying for position over the other and each certain that it alone had the wherewithal to put a period on the nation's controversies. The Marshall Court had done precisely this on behalf of the market revolution; the Taney Court, convinced that the executive and legislative branches had failed to resolve the slavery question, attempted to do so in 1857 and would very likely have done more had not the Civil War intervened. Not even the Emancipation Proclamation was necessarily exempt from Roger Taney's judicial veto. "Nobody expects," warned Orestes Brownson, "that the Supreme Court will sustain the freedom of slaves under the proclamation," particularly since (as Wendell Phillips sneered), Chief Justice Taney would read the proclamation "filtered through the secession heart of a man whose body was in Baltimore and whose soul was in Richmond."[27]

Lincoln's assertion of "war powers" that were beyond the Court's control (and with them, the general suspension by 1862 of the writ of *habeas corpus*) silenced much of what the Court might have tried to do in asserting its will. Clement Vallandigham's appeal to the Supreme Court in *ex parte Vallandigham* was denied simply because the Court held that it had no appellate jurisdiction over a military tribunal. But the appointment of a new chief justice to succeed Taney in 1864 and the end of hostilities seven months later let down the bars, and within a year the Supreme Court, starting with *ex parte Milligan,* had once more began drawing lines around executive and legislative authority. The primary intention of the Court may have been that of magnifying its office, or at least minimizing the role in Reconstruction exercised by the national legislature; nevertheless, the subsidiary result was to strike down executive and legislative initiatives on behalf of the freedpeople. "We have been, as a class, grievously wounded, wounded in the house of our friends," declared Frederick Douglass after *Civil Rights Cases,* "I look upon it as one more shocking development of that moral weakness in high places which has attended the conflict between the spirit of liberty and the spirit of slavery from the beginning. The whole essence of the thing is a studied purpose to degrade and stamp out the liberties of a race. It is the old spirit of slavery, and nothing else."[28]

Still, it has been said that Republicans themselves were as much to blame for this legal embezzlement as their rivals, for allowing themselves to listen so much to the blandishments of white racial reconciliation that their own hands weakened in the struggle. But the evidence for this yielding is mottled with contradictions. White Union veterans may have been more willing than they should have been to bury old military hatchets with white Confederates and to sign on to statements of mutual respect, as the survivors of great heroic moments. But the Union veterans were truer to the emancipation cause than they have been given credit for: the postwar Grand Army of the Republic memorialized its members "without distinction of race or creed," and the GAR would be one of the few postwar organizations which, as one black GAR member declared, "ignores the prejudice of race and regards as equally worthy all those who rendered the country service." And white officers who served with U.S. Colored Troops regiments during the war were some of black Americans' most unabashed defenders in the public sphere after the war.[29]

What is less well understood is the contradictory position African Americans themselves were forced to occupy in Reconstruction. The ideological core of the Republicans was based upon a free-labor ethic which glorified the small producer and the independent entrepreneur who was able to parlay a basic governmental encouragement—the "internal improvements" projects so beloved of the old Whig Party—into financial independence. This clash was not simply that of a Northern industrial capitalism with a premodern plantation economy, the chimera of the imaginations of the Progressive historians. The Northern economy, even during the Civil War, was far from the industrial behemoth that spawned the Progressives' counteraction; the average textile mill in 1869 employed fifty workers and the average manufacturing concern involved no more than fourteen. The Northern economy was as much a matter of a free-labor culture as it was dollars-and-cents. The genius of *free labor* was that it "makes all men equal; here the European noble and peasant work side-by-side." *Free labor* was "the highest honor of the system of government of the United States" because it embodied "the equal right of all men to the pursuit of happiness . . . the first natural and inalienable right." Free labor was "the right of every man over his own mind, heart, and body," declared Henry Ward Beecher, "over his time, movements, and relations to the physical world." Whether it made them rich or poor was beside the point; as Lincoln himself had said, free labor was what made the United States "the wonder and admiration of the whole world," because under the banner of free labor, "every man can make himself." It was not the triumph of corporate capitalism which Radical Republicans hoped to promote in the defeated South, but a bourgeois revolution in culture which would dig up the plantation "aristocracy" by the roots. The great offence of slavery, wrote Robert Dale Owen, the son of the famous utopian planner, was that it "breeds imperiousness of manner, impatience of contradiction or delay, ungovernable passion, contempt of labor" and "discourages enterprise . . . its tendency being to substitute these indolent fashions of dependence and luxurious self-indulgence"—all of them qualities which cut straight across the earnest expectations of bourgeois culture.[30]

So, not just the legal institution of slavery, but the entire culture which surrounded it had to go. "When England conquered the Highlands, she held them,—held them until she could educate them; and it took a generation," urged Wendell Phillips, the white Brahmin abolitionist. "That is just what we have to do with the South, annihilate the old South, and put a new one there." This new South's cultural vanguard would be a newly freed class of black wage laborers whose diligence and industry would allow them to save up enough cash to render themselves self-employed, and then still more successful to the point where they could hire others, and thus remake the entire social face of the South,

> Who, following in War's bloody trail,
> Shall every lingering wrong assail;
> All chains from limb and spirit strike,
> Uplift the black and white alike;
> Scatter before their swift advance
> The darkness and the ignorance,
> The pride, the lust, the squalid sloth,
> Which nurtured Treason's monstrous
>   growth,
> Made murder pastime, and the hell
> Of prison-torture possible;
> The cruel lie of caste refute,
> Old forms remould, and substitute
> For Slavery's lash the freeman's will,
> For blind routine, wise-handed skill;
> A school-house plant on every hill,

> Stretching in radiate nerve-lines thence
> The quick wires of intelligence;
> Till North and South together brought
> Shall own the same electric thought,
> In peace a common flag salute,
> And, side by side in labor's free
> And unresentful rivalry,
> Harvest the fields wherein they fought.[31]

Not only in the South, but even in the West, free-labor Republicanism would create a New England–style "high type" of culture: "the cultivated valley, the peaceful village, the church, the school-house, and thronging cities." Of course, with the reins of financial power restored to white Southern hands by Andrew Johnson's pardons, the freedpeople actually lacked the vital straps—the access to capital, the ownership of the means of production—to haul themselves by their own boots. What good did it do, the freedmen asked Whitelaw Reid, "to make them free, unless they were to own the land on which they had been working and which they had made productive and valuable." It was all well and good "to see even the New York *Herald* speak out vigorously for negro suffrage," Reid remarked, but without basic economic access, all hope of a *émbourgeoisement* of the freedmen, much less the South, was unlikely. "Gib us our own land and we take care of ourselves," pleaded one freedman, "widout land, de ole massas can hire us or starve us, as dey please."

But confiscation and redistribution, ironically, cut exactly across the face of bourgeois Republicanism. "At the South the white has for two hundred years robbed the black, and he is atoning for it to-day in sackcloth and ashes," editorialized the *Nation* in 1867. But "if we now set the black to rob the white, we may be sure that like retribution will speedily follow."

> The negro is just entering on free life, and if he is fit to vote . . . he is also fit to win a farm for himself as a poor white man has to win it. . . . A division of rich men's land amongst the landless, as the result of a triumph at the polls, would give a shock to our whole social and political system from which it would hardly recover without the loss of liberty. Every election would thenceforward threaten property, and men of property, we may be sure, would find, as they have found under similar circumstances in all countries, the means of protecting themselves—but not through constitutional government.

That, together with Johnson's pardons and the re-franchisement of the Southern elite, guaranteed that the South would remain the preserve of a cotton latifundia, and the emergence of an urban or industrial bourgeoisie would be anathema to Southern white elites. Former Confederates were incredulous at the suggestion that they should plow or keep shop themselves. When Carl Schurz suggested to a "Southern gentleman" that "he should work with his hands, as a farmer" or take up "some other business pursuit," the idea "seemed to strike him as ludicrously absurd. He told me with a smile that he had never done a day's work of that kind in his life." The white Southerners' task, the "gentleman" concluded, was to "make the nigger work somehow."[32]

And so, the bourgeois revolution failed—"the last revolutionary flicker that is strictly bourgeois and strictly capitalist"—and in the place of the plantation aristocracy came an agricultural serfdom based on sharecropping and the creation of a nonwage black peasantry that persisted into the twentieth century. When the black victims of this transformation called for still more federal intervention to compensate, the calls increasingly sounded in Republican ears like a fundamental betrayal of the free-labor principle, and more like the demands of populist farmers for currency inflation or unionized workers for economic regulation. As early as 1867, Illinois Republican Elihu Washburne was warned that, even though "the Republican Party have done a great work for the Negro . . . we should be satisfied for the present with what we have done, and protect him in the rights we have given him in those States where he was formerly a Slave and had no rights at all, but here we should stop. . . ." This was, in effect, to be punished for failing to live up to an ideal no one *could* have lived up to in the postwar South.[33]

But the freedpeople were not entirely the passive victims of a rigged game. As much as Theodore Tilton and Joel Prentiss Bishop assumed, a little too magisterially, that the way to a bright racial future lay in what amounted to the absorption of black people into whites, the freedpeople were distinctly less enthusiastic about surrendering an independent racial identity which they had forged under the most harrowing of circumstances. This preference became apparent, even before the end of 1865, in the creation of separate black religious denominations. Despite the resolution of the Georgia Conference of the Methodist Episcopal Church–South that "we are desirous that all our colored members should continue to be members of the M. E. Church, South," 95 percent of black Methodists left the churches of their former owners to establish their own; nor was this choice made merely out of fear that their onetime owners were attempting to extend the old regime through some form of new paternalism, since black church-goers rejected attachment to Northern abolitionist denominations as well. Anyone who imagined that former slaves were only waiting until emancipation to embrace lovingly their old masters had a very naïve view of slavery: "The feeling for the old slaveholders—whose rule was one of oppression and brutality—is no longer that of respect or awe; it is one of contempt and hatred." Black workers created their own unions, partly as a result of exclusion from white unions, but also as a means of seeking the dignity of a uniquely black labor. And they created their own fraternal organizations and paramilitary groups. In so doing, however, opportunities for alliances with broad swaths of anti-Confederate white Unionism disappeared.[34]

Nor were these problems limited to white-black suspicions; there was no shortage, either, of black-black suspicion. A racial hierarchy within African Americans of the South had long been in existence, with free blacks and "mulattoes" demanding higher seats at the banquet than freed slaves or dark-skinned

"Africans." Based on the evidence of fugitive slave advertisements in the decades before the Civil War, John Hope Franklin and Loren Schweninger estimated that at least 10 percent of the slave population were mixed-race by 1808, while the fugitive population was composed of as much as 43 percent mixed-race individuals, and after 1865, the divisions drawn by interracial difference became painfully apparent. "There is in the Southern States a great amount of prejudice in regards to color," William Wells Brown admitted in 1867, "even among the negroes themselves. The nearer the negro or mulatto approaches to the white, the more he seems to feel his superiority over those of a darker hue." The white South Carolina apologist, Edward Holland, praised "our Free Mulattoes" and was convinced that "in cases of insurrection," they were "more likely to enlist themselves under the banner of the whites" and "abhor the idea of association with blacks." It amazed the Illinois abolitionist Owen Lovejoy to find that, while it was no surprise that the free black population of Illinois was hostile to proposals for colonization, that hostility crumbled if "separate colonies" were to "be assigned to those of different shades of color," since the "objection" of the "colored people of the State" was that "blacks and mulattoes cannot live harmoniously together."[35]

Nor did this factionalism end with the war. Reconstruction Louisiana was disfigured by infighting among factions led by Pinckney Benton Stewart Pinchback (one-quarter black, and married to a white woman), Oscar James Dunn (born a slave, of a slave mother and a free black carpenter), and Caesar Carpentier Antoine (a onetime business partner of Pinchback's, whose father was a free *gens du couleur* and mother was West Indian). In postwar Mobile, free "mulatto" blacks, many of them Creole descendants of Mobile's onetime French and Spanish colonizers, quickly assumed dominance over newly freed slaves who flocked to the city from the fields. In postwar Savannah, the freedman Aaron Bradley mounted a political smear campaign against his rival for a seat in Congress, Richard White, a mixed-race Union Army veteran from Ohio. White, sneered Bradley, was a "hybrid" who did not deserve true African American votes. "What color will he represent himself?" asked Bradley. Answer: "The greasy color." Even Frederick Douglass and Martin Delany struck sparks, with Douglass (himself biracial) bitterly criticizing Delany's black racial purism for "going about the same length in favor of blacks, as the whites have done in favor of the doctrine of white superiority." Delany was right to assert African Americans' "need for dignity and self-respect," but not to point where "he stands up so straight that he leans back a little." These interracial feuds lay at the base of the most singular failure of black Reconstruction in the South, and that was the absence of a single commanding leader who could sum up the aspirations for equality and new racial order in his own forward example and bind together the disparate shards of African American identity into a single movement.[36]

But in a world come of age, it is easier to reduce these signs of historical complexity to more grimly monochrome proportions—easier, in other words, to lose confidence in the arc of justice, to regard *thine every flaw* as inherently unmendable, to see purposelessness and confusion, and assume malice. As Julius Lester wrote in 1968,

> One of the bigger lies that America has given the world is that Lincoln freed the slaves, and that blacks should be grateful from can to can't because Mr. Lincoln was so generous.... It is not true that Lincoln did so out of the goodness of his heart or that we have to be grateful to him.... The black school-child ... grows up

feeling half-guilty for even thinking about cussing out a white man, because he's been taught that it was a white man who gave us freedom. . . . What is the catechism the black child learns from Grade One on? "Class, what did Abraham Lincoln do?" "Lincoln freed the slaves," and the point is driven home that you'd still be down on Mr. Charlie's plantation working from can to can't if Mr. Lincoln hadn't done your great-great-grandmother a favor.

Coming of age does not necessarily mean *maturity;* there is a *faux*-maturation which comes of age in the loosening of trust, the reduction of causality to nothing-but, the confusion of nobility with perfection, the obliteration of American exceptionalism and its replacement with American deceptionalism—something which Lester unhappily confirmed when he celebrated the spirit of "resistance" in "the hustler who gambles, runs numbers, pushes drugs, lives off women, and does anything to avoid going to 'meet the man' five days a week, year in and year out," and all because this granted "a modicum of self-respect and the respect of a good segment of the community."[37]

So, is it really possible to break your own chains? Is it possible to splice moral debt so that some that

parts can be dismissed and the others held indefi-
nitely for collection? It is this dilemma which be-
clouds comprehension of the deed of emancipation
and the hatred of slavery manifest in one man,
Abraham Lincoln. It is to the dispelling of that cloud
which we must next turn.

2

THE ANTISLAVERY WORLD OF
ABRAHAM LINCOLN

I do not believe in the anti-slavery of Abraham
Lincoln, because he is on the side of this Slave
Power of which I am speaking, that has possession of the Federal Government. Now, two years
ago, I went through the State of Illinois for the
purpose of getting signers to a petition, asking
the Legislature to repeal the Testimony Law, so
as to permit colored men to testify against white
men. I went to prominent Republicans, and
among others to Abraham Lincoln and Lyman
Trumbull, and neither of them dared to sign
that petition, to give me the right to testify in a
court of justice! If we sent our children to school,
Abraham Lincoln would lick them out, in the
name of Republicanism and anti-slavery!

That was the judgment of the black Illinois abolitionist, Hezekiah Ford Douglass, in 1860, and he was

not alone in weighing Abraham Lincoln in the anti-slavery balances and finding him wanting. Wendell Phillips spoke at Tremont Temple in Boston the evening after Lincoln's election to the presidency and scoffed at the assumption that the rise of Abraham Lincoln meant any real change in national policy toward African Americans:

> Mark it, and let us question Mr. Lincoln about it.
>
> Do you believe, Mr. Abraham Lincoln, that the Negro is your political and social equal, or ought to be? Not a bit of it.
>
> Do you believe he should sit on juries? Never.
>
> Do you think he should vote? Certainly not.
>
> Should he be considered a citizen? I tell you frankly, no.
>
> Do you think that, when the declaration of Independence says, "All men are created equal," it intends the political equality of blacks and whites? No, sir.
>
> If this "idea that fills all generous minds" be equality, surely Mr. Lincoln's mind is yet empty. Do you see Mr. Lincoln? He believes a Negro

may walk where he wishes, eat what he earns, read what he can, and associate with any other who is exactly of the same shade of black he is. That is all he can grant.

So did William Lloyd Garrison a year later: "Mr. Lincoln is so infatuated as to shape his course of policy in accordance with their wishes, and is thus unwittingly helping to prolong the war, and to render the result more and more doubtful! If he is 6 feet 4 inches high, he is only a dwarf in mind." Even a political ally of Lincoln's—his attorney general, Edward Bates—unwittingly confirmed this skepticism on the eve of Lincoln's election in 1860, when he assured a correspondent who had asked him for his opinion of Lincoln and his probable course as president:

I think I know him very well, and I solemnly declare to you that, in my opinion, he is as true a conservative, national Whig as can be found in Missouri, Virginia or Tennessee (and that includes you and me and Mr. [John] Bell). He will fulfill his oath to the letter, by taking care that the laws (all the laws) be faithfully executed. He will studiously endeavor to restore peace and harmony; and to that end, will avoid as far as he can, all those exciting subjects which have so mischievously agitated the country, for some years past. He believes, as I do, that slavery in the states, belongs exclusively to the states that choose to have it; and that Congress has not, and ought not to have, any power over it there. And, as to the Territory, bought and conquered by the U. States, he believes, as I do, that Congress has full legislative power over it and may, at discretion, permit or forbid slavery therein.[1]

And it would not be difficult to continue piling up testimonies against Lincoln's bona fides as an enemy of slavery, even after he issued the Emancipation Proclamation, even after he signed the Thirteenth Amendment (which he was, after all, not constitutionally obliged to do), even after his murder led to the secular equivalent of beatification. The namesake of the Du Bois Institute, William Edward Burghardt Du Bois, said much the same thing as Phillips and Ford Douglass in 1917, in an address to the Intercollegiate Socialist Society, when he scoffed at calling Lincoln "the Emancipator." Lincoln's real "object was the integrity of the Union and not the emancipation of the slaves." If Lincoln "could keep the Union from being disrupted," Du Bois declared, "he would not only allow slavery to exist but would loyally protect it." Five years later, on the pages of the *Crisis,* he scorned Lincoln as "a Southern poor white, of illegitimate birth, poorly educated, and unusually ugly, awkward, ill-dressed," who was, at best, "inconsistent" for "despising Negroes and letting them fight and vote; protecting slavery and freeing slaves." Four months later, a popular outcry from the membership of the National Association for the Advancement of Colored People (NAACP) forced Du Bois to sugarcoat that scorn by insisting that he really did believe that "Abraham Lincoln was perhaps the greatest figure of the nineteenth century." But the sugarcoating was applied with reluctant thinness: Du Bois would "revere him" because of the way Lincoln, "despite the clinging smirch of low taste and shifty political methods, rose to be a great and good man and the noblest friend of the slave." By this means, Du Bois tried to suggest that his real problem with Lincoln was not race but class. Still, Du Bois never connected Lincoln's name to the Emancipation Proclamation, and in later years, he focused his attention instead on Lincoln's interest in colonization and compensated—which was to say, *halfhearted*—emancipation. This view of Lincoln was, ironically, just the same as that claimed by the white supremacists and segregationists whom Du Bois despised, but by the 1960s, this image of Lincoln was indeed the one that had taken shape in the black mind—that of "Abraham Lincoln . . . as a reactionary white supremacist."[2]

On the other hand, it is not difficult to deploy plenty of countervailing testimony. Joseph Gillespie, who was a Lincoln political confidante for two-and-a-half decades in Illinois, insisted that Lincoln grew "really excited" on the subject of slavery "and said with great earnestness that 'slavery was a great & crying injustice, an enormous national crime, and that we could not expect to escape punishment for it.'" In January 1861, George Julian visited Lincoln in Springfield to test for himself whether the president-elect's antislavery credentials were sound, and came away "gratified to find [Lincoln] less reserved and more emphatic than I expected. . . . Upon the whole . . . I was much pleased with our first Republican executive, and I returned home more fully inspired than ever with the purpose to sustain him to the utmost in facing the duties of his great office." Salmon Chase, the re-nowned "attorney general for fugitive slaves," also tested Lincoln on a visit to Springfield and came away satisfied that "all I hear of Lincoln implies confidence." Put no trust, he counseled an associate, "in the rumor that he will disappoint those who believe

William Edward Burghardt Du Bois, the foremost African American intellectual of his time and editor of the NAACP magazine, the *Crisis*. Du Bois scandalized readers of the *Crisis* in 1922 by criticizing Lincoln's sincerity as a "Great Emancipator."

Photograph by J. E. Purdy. *George Grantham Bain Collection, Library of Congress* in Republicanism." Emancipation, wrote Lincoln's fellow-Illinoisan and congressional ally, Isaac Newton Arnold, was Lincoln's "deepest, strongest desire of the soul," and from the time of his election Lincoln "hoped and expected to be the Liberator of the slaves." Even William Lloyd Garrison eventually embraced Lincoln as "an instrument in the hands of God to bring about great and glorious ends" and "to make no compromise with the dark spirit of slavery." Meeting Lincoln in 1864, the trumpeter of American abolition came away convinced that there could be "no mistake . . . in regard to Mr. Lincoln's desire to do all that he can see it right and possible for him to do to uproot slavery, and give fair play to the emancipated. I was much pleased with his spirit . . . and have no doubt of his thorough-going anti-slavery spirit and purpose."[3]

But multiplying these testimonies serves little purpose in the face of what Lincoln himself sometimes had to say. As often as he repeated his hostility to slavery—from his earliest declaration on the floor of the Illinois state legislature in 1837 that slavery constituted both "injustice and bad policy," through his repeated assertions in the 1850s that "I hate it because of the monstrous injustice of slavery itself," to his public declaration for Albert G. Hodges in 1864 that

"I am naturally anti-slavery" and "that if slavery is not wrong, nothing is wrong"—he can just as often be quoted expressing his skepticism about whether white Americans should concede any practical equality to blacks, civil or social.

One case in point was the great Peoria, Illinois, speech on October 16, 1854. He asked whether black slaves should be freed and made the equals of white people, and somewhat ambivalently answered *no:* "Free them, and make them politically and socially, our equals? My own feelings will not admit of this; and if mine would, we well know that those of the great mass of white people will not. Whether this feeling accords with justice and sound judgment, is not the sole question, if indeed, it is any part of it. A universal feeling, whether well or ill founded, can not be safely disregarded. We can not, then, make them equals."

Another instance occurred at the beginning of his senatorial campaign against Stephen A. Douglas in July 1858, when Lincoln announced that "last night Judge Douglas tormented himself with horrors about my disposition to make negroes perfectly equal with white men in social and political relations." Lincoln neither embraced nor denied the assertion, but instead denied that he had ever said such a thing, and from there, added ambiguously, "I adhere to the Declaration of Independence. If Judge Douglas and his friends are not willing to stand by it, let them come up and amend it."

Then in the opening debate in his famous series with Douglas that fall, Lincoln stated that "anything that argues me into his idea of perfect social and political equality with the negro, is but a specious and fantastic arrangement of words, by which a man can prove a horse chestnut to be a chestnut horse." And even though he inserted the qualifier *probably* to describe the permanence of white supremacy, nevertheless he suggested that, at least pragmatically, he had no objection to being considered a black man's racial superior. "There is a physical difference between the two, which in my judgment will probably forever forbid their living together upon the footing of perfect equality, and inasmuch as it becomes a necessity that there must be a difference, I, as well as Judge Douglas, am in favor of the race to which I belong, having the superior position."

And not even Dr. Alexandre Manette could have been saddled with a greater self-condemnation than the one Lincoln expressed, apparently spontaneously, at the beginning of his fourth debate with Stephen A. Douglas at Charleston, Illinois, in 1858:

Lincoln at the time of the Lincoln-Douglas debates in 1858, as depicted by Andrew O'Connor for the Illinois State Capitol, Springfield, Illinois, in 1918.

Author's collection

I am not, nor ever have been, in favor of
bringing about in any way the social and
political equality of the white and black races,
that I am not nor ever have been in favor of
making voters or jurors of negroes, nor of
qualifying them to hold office, nor to intermarry with white people; and I will say in
addition to this that there is a physical difference between the white and black races which I
believe will forever forbid the two races living
together on terms of social and political equality.
And in as much as they cannot so live, while
they do remain together there must be the
position of superior and inferior, and I as much
as any other man am in favor of having the
superior position assigned to the white race.

And so, we conclude with a satisfied sigh, Ford
Douglass was right, after all. It was these words
which drove Lerone Bennett, as a young man in Mississippi, to abandon any loyalty, any sense of debt
or obligation as a black man, to Abraham Lincoln.
"I was just—just absolutely shocked," Bennett told
Brian Lamb in 2000, "because I find it difficult to
understand how people could say this man was the

greatest apostle of . . . brotherhood in the United States of America."[4]

I suspect, however, that Bennett's shock was accompanied by a measure of relief. As children, we admire our parents as the greatest and best human beings who tread the earth; as adolescents and adults, with independent identities to maintain, our estimate is more measured, and though adolescence tends to be more harsh in its judgments than adulthood, we will still shift a little uncomfortably to think that we are our father's sons, or that *they all turn out like their mothers.* In a noteworthy essay on why he could not enter into celebrations of Juneteenth, John McWhorter complained, "I just can't wrap my head around celebrating the fact that someone else freed my ancestors," much less that "freedom happened partly as the result of whites making other whites see the error of their ways. . . . I am always more interested in what we did rather than what somebody did to us."[5] To come of age is to *put away childish things,* and not always because we have outgrown them, or because they never were anything but childish, but because we *must,* because we are *obliged* to be adults. It is also pointless to attempt (as we are often prone to do in moments of sentimental weakness) a reversal to which we have not given free assent. But we *are* obliged, if truth has any meaning, separate the struggle to come of age from apologetics, if only in the interest of our own epistemological self-awareness.

To begin with, there is no good reason to doubt the sincerity of Lincoln's declarations of hatred for slavery. Fundamental to all his notions of political life was the American Declaration of Independence, and within that, its announcement that "all men are created equal." This was the fundamental "proposition" to which he believed the American republic was dedicated, "held sacred by all, and thought to include all." It was the "standard maxim for free society," the "stumbling block" which, no matter how imperfectly developed at any given time, was still sufficient in itself to ruin the plans of all "those who in after times might seek to turn a free people back into the hateful paths of despotism." But in what respect were all men created *equal*? "I think the authors of that notable instrument . . . did not intend to declare all men equal in all respects," Lincoln explained in 1857. "They did not mean to say all were equal in color, size, intellect, moral developments, or social capacity," any more than we could imagine that equality demands to-day, in the spirit of Kurt Vonnegut Jr.'s Harrison Bergeron, that we pursue a state "not only equal before God and the law" but "equal every which way." But they did lay out "with tolerable distinctness, in what respects they did consider all men created equal—equal in 'certain inalienable rights, among which are life, liberty, and the pursuit of happiness.' This they said, and this meant."[6]

What Lincoln would probably have to explain to us, for whom the notion of inalienable rights is inalienably remote, is this: every human being, universally, is born into this world with certain physical attributes and certain moral attributes which are as inalterable and essential to any worthwhile definition of humanity as a trunk is to an elephant, or a crest to a blue jay. Among those moral attributes are the natural rights Jefferson—and Lincoln—itemized: *life, liberty,* and *the pursuit of happiness.* Without these, we are something less than human; and when someone attempts to deprive us of them, our natural instinct is to fight back. These natural rights are shared irrespective of one's nationality, color, race, language, ethnicity, or, for that matter, anything else which acts to particularize one person over against another. Hence, "men who have come from Europe"—or anywhere else, for that matter—and "settled here" may

have no genealogical connection at all to the American founders; "but when they look through that old
Declaration of Independence, they find that those old
men say that 'We hold these truths to be self-evident,
that all men are created equal,'" and at that moment
"they feel that that moral sentiment taught in that
day evidences their relation to those men, that it is the
father of all moral principle in them, and that they
have a right to claim it as though they were blood
of the blood, and flesh of the flesh of the men who
wrote that Declaration, and so they are." In fact, the
instinctive recognition of natural right embraced
more than just the human race: "all feel and understand it, even down to brutes and creeping insects."
Even "the ant, who has toiled and dragged a crumb
to his nest, will furiously defend the fruit of his
labor, against whatever robber assails him." How
more natural was it, then, for the black slave to "con-
stantly know that he is wronged" by slavery.[7]

In systematic fashion, slavery robbed the slave of
liberty, by robbing him of the most elementary of
rights, which was *agency*. "When the white man governs himself that is self-government," by all of Lincoln's understanding of democracy and free labor; on
the other hand, "when he governs himself, and also
governs another man" without that other's consent,

"that is despotism." Hence, "if the negro is a man, why then my ancient faith teaches me that 'all men are created equal;' and that there can be no moral right in connection with one man's making a slave of another." Of course, slaveholders might counter with the argument that a black slave was not really human at all, but some entirely different and subordinate species, in the style of Karl Vogt; but if that were the case, Lincoln said, it was certainly passing strange that there should be "400,000 free negroes in the United States," worth, at the slaveholders' valuation, near $2 million. Who, in their right mind, would allow $2 million-worth of horses, cattle, or sheep—"two million dollars worth of any other kind of property—running about without an owner?" Yet, there are 400,000 free blacks "running about" without masters. And why? because they *can* be free—because they are men, not things, with "mind, feeling, souls, family affections, hopes, joys, sorrows—something that made them more than hogs or horses." Simply by showing themselves capable of *liberty,* black men *by* their liberty show that they are the natural equals of every other man in creation and therefore deserve freedom, and not slavery.[8]

Slavery next robbed the slave of the *pursuit of happiness,* because it extinguished any hope on the part of the slave of self-betterment. "The condition of the negro slave in America," wrote Lincoln in 1855, is, simply by virtue of being a slave, as "fixed, and hopeless of change for the better, as that of the lost souls of the finally impenitent." Just as no proposition moved Lincoln's political mind more than Jefferson's "proposition" of inalienable rights, no prospect moved Lincoln's economic mind more than what Gabor Boritt has called "the right to rise." The genius of the American republic lay not its "frowning battlements, our bristling sea coasts, the guns of our war steamers, or the strength of our gallant and disciplined army," but in its economic open-endedness, in the mobility of free labor. In this republic, unlike the monarchies of the Old World or the castes of Asia, "we proposed to give all a chance; and we expected the weak to grow stronger, the ignorant, wiser; and all better, and happier together." No American began life, handicapped by some ancient status, inherited from generations out of mind. "There is no permanent class of hired laborers amongst us." Lincoln himself was "not ashamed to confess that twenty five years ago I was a hired laborer, mauling rails, at work on a flat boat—just what might happen to any poor man's son." So, "when one starts poor, as most do in the race of life," the principal virtue of "free society" is that "he knows he can better his condition; he knows that there is no fixed condition of labor, for his whole life." He can "acquire property as fast as he can ... get wealthy" and enjoy "an equal chance to get rich with everybody else." That

> men who are industrious, and sober, and honest in the pursuit of their own interests should after a while accumulate capital, and after that should be allowed to enjoy it in peace, and also if they should choose when they have accumulated it to use it to save themselves from actual labor and hire other people to labor for them is right. In doing so they do not wrong the man they employ, for they find men who have not of their own land to work upon, or shops to work in, and who are benefited by working for others, hired laborers, receiving their capital for it. Thus a few men that own capital, hire a few others, and these establish the relation of capital and labor rightfully.

The key word for Lincoln in describing this environment is *industrious*—not, significantly, *white* or *black*. And however naïve it may strike us today, in a world of global corporations, to imagine that capitalist relations are created by *a few men* hiring *a few men,* it was nevertheless the environment in which Lincoln lived, and indeed, the one which described his own life. The pursuit of happiness impelled Lincoln to "want every man to have the chance," and, as he added in 1860, "I believe a black man is entitled to it—

"Lincoln as a Flatboatman on the Mississippi River," a campaign poster from 1860 emphasizing Lincoln's common-man origins as a laborer and the opportunities for self-improvement in a free-labor economy. In 1860, Lincoln said, "I am not ashamed to confess that twenty-five years ago I was a hired laborer, mauling rails, at work on a flat-boat—just what might happen to any poor man's son. I want every man to have the chance—and I believe a black man is entitled to it—in which he can better his condition." The sixth debate in the Lincoln-Douglas debates took place in Quincy, Illinois, in 1858.

Library of Congress

in which he can better his condition—when he may look forward and hope to be a hired laborer this year and the next, work for himself afterward, and finally to hire men to work for him!"[9]

At its ultimate extension, slavery robbed the slave of *life,* first by stripping him of everything his life had produced, and, if the master so willed, killing him at the first sign of rebellion. "I confess I hate to see the poor creatures hunted down, and caught, and carried back to their stripes, and unrewarded toils." As he told his lifelong friend, Joshua Speed, in 1855, slavery's power over the lives of its victims "was a continual torment to me; and I see something like it every time I touch the Ohio, or any other slave border." And being "carried back" to slavery was only the beginning of the slave's torments. In the shadow of slavery, Lincoln knew that even a free black man—in 1837, it was a "mulatto man, by the name of McIntosh," in St. Louis—could be "seized in the street, dragged to the suburbs of the city, chained to a tree, and actually burned to death; and all within a single hour from the time he had been . . . attending to his own business, and at peace with the world." Death haunted Lincoln's dreams, his presidency, his family, even his occasional stabs at poetry, and always, his policies. "I reckon there never was a man raised in the country, on a farm . . . that ever grew up with such an aversion to bloodshed as I have," Lincoln told Illinois congressman Henry Bromwell, "and yet I've had more questions of life and death to settle in four years than all the men who ever sat in this chair put together."[10] Taken together, these multiple violations of natural law were more than enough to drive Lincoln into antislavery activism in the 1850s and to make him the first antislavery president.

The problem with our apprehension of Lincoln's antislavery is that he seems to have gone about it in what we would regard as a bafflingly obtuse fashion. There is, to begin with, almost no concern with slavery as a matter of *race*. Lincoln saw slavery as an "issue . . . most distinctly joined on the point of the rights of labor," as a "struggle for the rights of labor, and for the form of government by which alone those rights can be securely maintained." Slavery, he told Joseph Gillespie, is

> "the most glittering ostentatious & displaying
> property in the world and now[,]" says he[,] "if a
> young man goes courting the only inquiry is
> how many negroes he or she owns and not what

other property they may have[.]" The love for Slave property was swallowing up every other mercenary passion[.] Its ownership betokened not only the possession of wealth but indicated the gentleman of leisure who was above and scorned labour[.] These things Mr[.] Lincoln regarded as highly seductive to the thoughtless and giddy headed young men who looked upon work as vulgar and ungentlemanly.

We could, in fact, read a great deal of Lincoln's comments and speeches on slavery—even the Emancipation Proclamation—without having any notion that the slaves he was proposing to emancipate were *black,* or that American slavery had always been almost exclusively a matter of enslaving the members of one race. His description of the "continual torment" imposed by the sight of "the poor creatures, hunted down, and caught, and carried back to their stripes," is almost the only description in the eight volumes that make up Lincoln's collected writings which approaches empathy for the slave as *black*. Slavery, for Lincoln, was a *political* and *economic* problem before it was a *racial* one, and there were moments when it seemed as though his determination to end slavery was a determination to end it as a threat to white people. He was forthright in claiming that the Declaration of Independence—"this Charter of Freedom"—applied to "the slave as well as to ourselves," but the real danger posed by slavery's defenders was that "class of arguments put forward to batter down that idea, are also calculated to break down the very idea of a free government, even for white men." Slaveholders in their "greedy chase to make profit of the negro" angered Lincoln—not out of sympathy for "the negro," but because that chase would lead them to "cancel and tear to pieces even the white man's charter of freedom." His opposition to the expansion of slavery into the western territories, which became his principal brief against slavery in the 1850s, was, in practice, *more* racially exclusive than slavery, since he was quite frank in stating that he wanted slavery banned from the territories because "we want them for the homes of free white people. This they cannot be, to any considerable extent, if slavery shall be planted within them." And not only free white Americans; the territories had to be restricted for free settlement "as an outlet for free white people everywhere, the world over." Nor was Lincoln articulating a view considered in any way unusual, even among the most advanced abolitionists. James Ashley, who would be the floor leader responsible for managing the Thirteenth Amendment through the House of Representatives, was happy to claim in 1860 that "it is the purpose and mission of the Republican party to . . . provide a way for the final separation of the two races. . . . The policy of the Republican party is, by an ultimate separation of the two races, to secure the liberty and happiness of both."[11]

But if we are struck by Lincoln's lack of racial empathy, we also are looking at the wrong man for expressions of empathy on almost any subject. This was a man, as William Herndon warned Joseph Gillespie, whose "great good Common Sense came to him not through his judgments, but through his reasoning. . . . Some men get this Common Sense as it were by inspiration—catch it by lightning . . . not so Lincoln. Lincoln's common sense Came through his brain and not through his Soul." Lincoln had an almost Vulcan preoccupation with logic, a shrinking from Romantic sensibility that reminds us more of the eighteenth than the nineteenth century. "It is thought by some men that Mr. Lincoln was a very warm-hearted man, spontaneous and impulsive," reflected Herndon. "This is not the exact truth." On a day-to-day basis, "Lincoln was not a very social man. He was not spontaneous in his feelings; was, as some said, rather cold." In his fourteen years of law practice with Lincoln, Herndon came to see him as a man with "relatively no imagination and no fancy" and "purely logical," whose "perceptions were slow, cold, precise, and exact" and who "followed his conclusions to the ultimate end, though the world perished." It would be, for Abraham Lincoln, a "happy day, when, all appetites controlled, all passions subdued, all matters subjected, mind, all conquering mind, shall live and move the monarch of the world."[12]

Chilly as this devotion to reason seems to us, it may lose some its less forbidding aspect when we remember that Romantic empathy of the sort that wept over Uncle Tom and Little Eva also invented the vast sludge of a racist "Divine economy," of organic nationalism, of folk tales and Teutonic forests, of Aryan blood and native soil. When Lincoln proposed colonization as the next step beyond emancipation, it did not spring from mysterious invocations of racial superiority, but from a hard-boiled calculation of political likelihoods. "Your race are suffering, in my judgment, the greatest wrong inflicted on any people," he said to the delegation of African American clergy whom he brought to the White House in August, 1862—which, by itself, may have been the most remarkable admission any president had ever made on the subject of race up till that time. Nor did he rise from that in defense or excuse of white people. "I do not know how much attachment you may have toward our race. It does not strike me that you have the greatest reason to love them." In the world of Romantic enthusiasm, Lincoln might well have been advised to move ahead with emancipation without impeaching his proclamation over discussions of colonization, and let white people chew their carpets as they liked, so long as justice was done. But Lincoln was wary of enthusiasm, and especially the enthusiasm which responded to the racial challenge of emancipation with the prescription *fiat justitia ruat caelum*—do right though the heavens fall. Years before, Lincoln rejected the idea that people should do their duty and leave the consequences to God, as "merely . . . an excuse for taking a course that they were not able to maintain by a fair and full argument." If there was no place in political morality "for judgment, we might as well be made without intellect." Consequently, he could not merely take up the pen to emancipate, without at the same time counting the cost. "Even when you cease to be slaves," Lincoln advised the African American pastors, "you are yet far removed from being placed on an equality with the white race," and he had very little authority to do anything about that. There was no metaphysics to this, and so he did "not propose to discuss this, but to present it as a fact with which we have to deal." Hence, they should consider colonization. "Lincoln's whole life," said his longtime legal associate Leonard Swett, "was a calculation of the law of forces, and ultimate results." The forces might be unjust, and everyone might know that they were unjust, but there they were.

> The world to him was a question of cause and effect. He believed the results to which certain causes tended, would surely follow; he did not believe that those results could be materially hastened, or impeded. His whole political history, especially since the agitation of the Slavery question, has been based upon this theory.[13]

But, by that very line of thinking, *race* was for Lincoln a fundamentally irrational consideration. It was true that he could "not alter it if I would" and that it "is a fact" lodged in American cultural perceptions. But, curiously, it was also a fact which he told the pastors' delegation "about which we all think and feel alike, I and you." Lincoln was, after all, the first president to invite black men to a public consultation on

Lincoln sat for this photograph by Polycarpus von Schneidau, a Chicago daguerreotypist, at the time of his first, unsuccessful run for the U.S. Senate in 1854.

Library of Congress

race policy—even if their participation was limited to listening to *him* speak—and it could certainly have given the nickel-plated variety of white supremacist little comfort to learn that Lincoln had welcomed them to the White House, "shaking hands very cordially with each one." If he doubted out loud in 1858 the wisdom of "bringing about in any way the social and political equality of the white and black races," he did so because in Illinois, the deck of civil rights had been stacked high against such equality—and in a democracy, societies have the right to determine what civil privileges they will confer upon whom. He was "not, nor ever have been, in favor" of such an equality; what he did not say was that he was inalterably opposed to it ever happening. If "there must be the position of superior and inferior," he added, then "I as much as any other man am in favor of having the superior position assigned to the white race," but he did not exegete that peculiar qualifier *as much as any other man,* and he would "say there is no such necessary conflict. I say that there is room enough for us all to be free." Certainly, in the possession of natural rights—"the right to eat the bread, without leave of anybody else, which his own hand earns," Lincoln explained—the black man "is my equal and the equal . . . of every living man." That was what the Declaration of Independence proclaimed, and he was confident, not only that the "declaration of equality of natural rights among all nations is correct," but that "no sane man will attempt to deny that the African upon his own soil has all the natural rights that instrument vouchsafes to all mankind." On that basis, Lincoln proposed, let us consider, as did John Henry, that *a man ain't nothin' but a man.* "Let us discard all this quibbling about this man and the other man—this race and that race and the other race—being inferior, and therefore they must be placed in an inferior position . . . and unite as one people throughout this land, until we shall once more stand up declaring that all men are created equal."[14]

The distinction Lincoln drew between natural rights and civil or political or social rights had specific meaning in his day. All men are created naturally and inalterably equal, but political rights are of a lesser order, are amendable to change, and are assigned by communities. "All men are not equally entitled to political rights," wrote the eminent historian George Park Fisher in 1864. "Slavery can be abolished, and yet the right of suffrage be withheld, or granted, at the discretion of the community, as a free reward of industry and intelligence." If voting (or any other political right) "were a natural, inborn, universal right," then there would be no sense or justice in "the limiting of the privilege of voting" to those "who shall have reached the age of twenty-one years." On the same logic, Lincoln could preach both universal natural equality—and demand the abolition of slavery as a violation of the natural right to liberty—without feeling any contradiction in suggesting that the freedpeople did not necessarily acquire political equality at the same time. What is significant is (a) the fundamental insistence on natural equality, which was far more than white supremacists like Stephen A. Douglas were willing to grant, and (b) the open-ended possibility that, in a democratic society, minds that withheld political rights at one moment might at another be persuaded to grant them. And he himself was, again, his own best example. He signed the legislation that extended diplomatic reciprocity to the world's two black republics, Haiti and Liberia. And although as president he had no standing by which to dictate the voting laws of reconstructed Louisiana, the testimony of the black soldier in the Civil War was sufficient for him (in the last speech he gave, on the evening of April 11, 1865) to urge the extension of "the elective franchise ... to the colored man," especially "the very intelligent, and on those who serve our cause as soldiers." This does not strike people today as the upper limit of generosity. But it was as much as a president could recommend in 1865; and it was enough to make one of his hearers that night, John Wilkes Booth, conclude that "that means nigger citizenship. Now, by God! I'll put him through. That is the last speech he will ever make."[15]

Yet, I suspect, not a syllable of this pleading persuades anyone today. Epistemological self-awareness involves risks which threaten the simplicity with which the self strives to live in a world come of age. In the passion to assert that "justice in our courts, earnings on our jobs, whether we have a job at all, the quality of our life, the means and timing of our death—all form a stacked deck every child born black must take up to play the game of life," it becomes possible to forget how many *Southern* whites fought Jim Crow, even in Jim Crow's darkest hours, or how Virginia was governed by a biracial coalition of "Readjusters," led by a Confederate general, in the 1870s and 1880s. The history of race from emancipation to segregation is by no means a predictable or a straight one, leading inexorably downward.[16]

The most significant example of how simplicity crowds out complexity in this history is reparations, or rather the demand for legal or congressional action to create financial reparations for the enslavement of modern African Americans' ancestors. In a sensational lead article in the May 2014 issue of the *Atlantic,* Ta-Nehisi Coates writes that slavery "was not incidental to America's rise; it facilitated that rise. By erecting a slave society, America created the economic foundation for its great experiment in democracy." Coates argues that "closing the 'achievement gap' will do nothing to close the 'injury gap'"; hence, "Reparations would seek to close this chasm." It would be costly: Coates cites an estimate drawn from Boris Bittker's *The Case for Black Reparations* (1973) that pegs the amount at $34 billion (in 1973 dollars). But Coates is skeptical about the possibilities—not because of the price tag, but because "white supremacy is not merely the work of hotheaded demagogues, or a matter of false consciousness, but a force so fundamental to America that it is difficult to imagine the country without it." Reparations would require Americans "to imagine a new country." And, one suspects, in the new "collective biography" reparations would create, there would be scant room for Abraham Lincoln.[17]

Coates' skepticism may run deeper than it needs to, though. Reparations for historical harms is not by any means a new idea. Payments in compensation for lost life or property have held an ever-growing place in international law since the Napoleonic Wars, when the confiscation and destruction of commerce and culture reached proportions so epidemic that the Congress of Vienna was compelled to demand, for the first time in modern history, the repatriation of the vast array of cultural artifacts and treasure seized wholesale by Napoleon Bonaparte and his armies. In 1865, General William T. Sherman's Special Field Order No. 15 divided the lands of former slaveholders in the Carolinas into forty-acre plots for newly freed slaves in the Carolinas, and Tennessee's Freedmen's Bureau superintendent, Clinton Fisk, expected "at no distant day" to see every freedman given "twenty, thirty, or forty acres of land, a mule or two, seeds and hoes, a cabin with his own family therein, a school-house for him and his, near by, and *freedom.*" A reparations bill was actually introduced into Congress by Thaddeus Stevens in March 1867. The Southern Homestead Act of 1866 opened-up over 45 million acres of public land in five Southern states to "loyal" whites and blacks alike (although by 1869, only 4,000 blacks had filed claims for it). The promise of "forty acres and a mule" made by General Sherman was taken up repeatedly by African American leaders like Ernest Lyon, who used the opportunity of an

Emancipation Day address in 1913 to demand the United States "purge itself of this breach of promise by paying the bill, with legal interest; if not, according to the legal terms of the agreement . . . then in its just equivalents, either by pensioning the survivors of the slave system . . . or by a liberal grant of money to the schools of the land charged with the educational development of their much proscribed posterity." In his pathbreaking 1993 essay on African American reparations, Vincene Verdun identified nothing less than five separate waves of reparations activism since 1863, beginning with Reconstruction and culminating in the current surge of interest which began in January 1989, when John Conyers first introduced congressional legislation for a Commission to Study Reparation Proposals for African Americans Act.[18]

This activism has not meant, however, that reparations have been reduced merely to a question of *when* rather than *if*. Reparations encode a series of tricky interpretive variables which Thomas Berger analyzes in terms of four categories: official memory (government-mandated narratives of the past), historical determinism (narratives are dictated purely by "what actually happened"), instrumentalism (where narratives become political creations shaped for the achievement of living political agendas), and culturalist (narratives of the past cannot be constructed apart from understanding cultural cues). This means that any narrative which supports, or deplores, the extraction of reparations has to be examined for its own presuppositions, entirely apart from the commonsense appearance of demanding tit for tat. For instance: if a narrative points toward victims as the proper recipients of reparations, the question of what constitutes a *victim* suddenly becomes vital— and nearly impossible to determine. Numerous ethnic and political groups have been victimized over the course of recent history by forced removal, genocide, confiscation, and ethnic cleansing, but some of them are unlikely to receive anything in the way of reparations. (I am thinking of the Sudeten Germans displaced by the Czechs, and the Silesian and Pomeranian Germans expelled by the new Polish government at the end of the Second World War, as well as the Greeks forcibly relocated by the Turks from Asia Minor in 1921–1923, and the survivors of the Armenian genocide of 1915.)[19]

Nor are all offers of reparations worth taking. Many reparations proposals for slavery were deeply tinged with racial paternalism. William H. Kimball, an abolitionist writing in 1864, insisted that the United States could not discharge its debt to the newly freed slaves merely by declaring them free. "To unloose the chains that have bound them, and set them adrift to contend and compete under our methods of individualism or isolated interests, is to doom them to conditions hardly to be preferred to those from which they are about to escape." But the reparations Kimball proposed as the remedy for that situation were largely a strategy for control of the freed slaves and were based on his perception of blacks as "a people in a state of infantile weakness and inexperience; whom, from the irrepressible laws and conditions of the human mind, we must govern and control, either wisely and beneficently or otherwise." The abolitionist vanguard in the Civil War Congress—Henry Wilson, Thaddeus Stevens, George Julian, Charles Sumner, Lyman Trumbull—advocated setting aside land seized from rebel landowners for homesteading by Union soldiers and sailors. But their proposal involved land distribution to black *and* white veterans, without reference to slavery. George Boutwell advocated forced removal of the white population of South Carolina and Florida, and turning these states over to the freed slaves. But Boutwell's proposal sounded very much like the creation of covert Bantustans (the supposedly independent black states created by the South African apartheid regime), and it found few backers even among African Americans. Other Northerners perceived post–Civil War reparations as payments that might be demanded, not by the former slaves, but by the former *slave owners,* as compensation for the loss of their capital investment in slaves. "There may be some danger, as the years go by," warned Maine congressman James Blaine in 1866, that "the people of the South whom were in rebellion, feeling the loss of their slaves and, perhaps, the poverty and hardship that resulted from that loss, will ask for some remuneration from the conquering Government."[20]

Reparations proposals of the sort called for by Coates are also plagued by questions concerning the precise *strategy* for obtaining reparations. John Conyers, with whom Coates sympathizes, has always believed that the path most likely to lead to success lies through legislative action. But in the 1990s, as big-time litigators won enormous payouts, and enormous headlines, by prying $206 billion from the nation's four largest tobacco companies, litigation became the new weapon of choice—most dramatically in 2002, in a federal lawsuit was filed in federal district court in Brooklyn by a group headed by Deadria Farmer-Paellmann, Edward Fagan, and Robert Wareham against FleetBoston Financial, the insurance giant Aetna, and CSX "to determine proper restitution, with reparations" from FleetBoston, CSX and Aetna for their complicity in insuring or employing slave labor before the Civil War.[21]

This contest between legislation and litigation has come to involve more than merely a disagreement among friends about who has a better map. The litigation option (with its overtones of combat and confrontation) enjoys a number of satisfying valences with black nationalism, while the legislative option strikes its critics as too much of an accommodation to a political system which has yielded a history of oppression and neglect. In that respect, the disagreement over reparations strategy has become the newest form, among African Americans, of the struggle over integration and separation. James Forman was candid about this in 1969: "Reparations did not represent any kind of long-range goal to our minds.... We saw it as a politically correct step" which "would not merely involve money but would be a call for revolutionary action." But what this view implies is that reparations litigation is actually a means rather than an end, a kind of performative theater where the performers have no real concern or expectation that there will be results, only a fresh extension of grievance.[22]

Whatever cultural dividends a courtroom show-down over reparations might yield, it is not likely to result in any concrete rewards for African Americans; what is worse, the proponents of the litigation option may persist in that path precisely because the cultural dividends are in fact more clearly desirable than the possible legal verdict. If we are in any sense serious about reparations for slavery, our first concern and our guiding star must be *cui bono*—who benefits? Asking any other question means that we have no moral grip on what reparations should mean. "Racial reconciliation," writes Roy L. Brooks, "should be the primary purpose of slave redress," and indeed that is partly why Coates compares reparations to "an airing of family secrets, a settling with old ghosts...a healing of the American psyche and the banishment of white guilt.[23] But reconciliation is not what reparations litigation is likely to produce, and largely for three reasons:

Who should the defendants be? The Farmer-Paellmann suit would seem to have settled that question by pursuing modern corporations with long and identifiable historic roots in the soil of slavery. The limitation there, however, is that even deep-pocket corporations like Aetna cannot fill the bill demanded by reparations. The "Millions for Reparations" march in August 2002 had a more lucrative target in view, and that was the United States government. "This is the first time there has been a mass rally demanding reparations from the United States government," said Conrad Worrill of the National Black United Front at the march, "They owe us!" And beyond that, there must surely be a day of reckoning for the international banking houses that provided much of the capital that funded Americans' purchase of slaves and played a major role in monetizing, commodifying and collateralizing slaves.[24]

But in the case of the U.S. government, the litigation strategy has to come to terms with the doctrine of sovereign immunity, and sovereign immunity was at the heart of the failure of an earlier reparations law suit, *Cato v. United States* in December 1995. A second roadblock to litigating against the federal government is less well known, largely because it occurs in a less-well-known place in the Constitution, and that is Article I, Section 9's ban on bills of attainder. Translated into modern legal English, a ban on attainder means a ban on any effort to punish an individual or group of individuals who have not actually been found guilty of a crime by a court, and under the definition of "punish," the Supreme Court has made it clear that it means monetary or property retribution, not just apologies or expressions of remorse. This obstacle, in turn, points to a third problem in filing a suit directed at the federal government, and that is the absence of statutory culpability. Slavery was legally recognized and codified in United States from 1789 till 1865 as a result of individual state statutes— it was never recognized or codified by the United States, which is a point easy to forget unless we realize what a thick line was drawn between federal and state jurisdictions until well into the twentieth century. It was the slave states which made slavery legal, just as the free states made themselves free between 1780 and 1827 by state enactments. By the time of the Civil War, apologists for slavery candidly boasted that the slaveholding South had never "even been aided by the Federal Government" in the creation of a slave society. "We have neither sought from it, protection for our private pursuits, nor appropriations for our public improvements."[25]

At only two other points did the federal government touch on slavery as a legal entity, and that concerned (a) the rendition of fugitives, which was codified first in 1793 and then again in 1850, and (b) slavery in the District of Columbia and the western territories. If a law suit against the United States for reparations is to go forward, it will have to build upon the comparatively poor materials of the Fugitive Slave Laws and filed in the name of only those descendants of slaves who were held in the District of Columbia before district emancipation occurred in April 1862. The federal government, as George Shedler has patiently pointed out, "neither owned nor traded in slaves and had no fruits of the practice to disgorge."[26]

That does, however, raise the possibility that individual states could be litigated against. But again, there are difficulties to be recognized beforehand. The most unnerving problem involves a question that usually does not surface at first thought, and that is, *which states?* When one thinks of slavery at the state level, the mind turns naturally to the eleven states which constituted the Confederacy, and perhaps also the four border states of Maryland, Delaware, Kentucky, and Missouri which stayed in the Union. But in fact, if we take matters back beyond the American Revolution, slavery was legal in every one of the thirteen British colonies which became the United States. In Connecticut, a state usually associated with New England abolitionism, slavery was not wiped off the statute books until 1848.[27] If Alabama is to be sued, is there not also an obligation to sue Illinois? Is Pennsylvania less culpable for ninety-eight years of slavery than Alabama for eighty-nine years (when the territory which was later organized as Alabama was obtained by cession from the British in the 1783 Treaty of Paris)? This point brings us to the second great question concerning reparations litigation.

Who should be the plaintiffs? This at first would seem so obvious as not to be worth asking: African Americans, of course. But determinations of ethnic guilt or innocence are much more slippery than they may at first appear. And in the case of African Americans, a difficulty for basing reparations awards on ethnic identity lurks in the genes of the very African Americans seeking to file such suits, and that is the widespread history of forced rape and violent sexual exploitation across the entire slave South. White males used and abused generations of defenseless black women as sexual toys, and the offspring of these unions were themselves doomed to enslavement and exploitation. Consequently, an entire population of African Americans has passed down to its descendants a generous mixing of the gene pool of Europe as well as of Africa. Even in the notorious case of Thomas Jefferson and Sally Hemings, Hemings herself was the daughter of Jefferson's father-in-law and a slave woman, and was so much a blend of black and white that, after Jefferson's death, she was classified as "white" by a census taker in Charlottesville; at least two of her children were sufficiently light-skinned that they "passed" into white society. In fact, almost any American family with at least a few generations behind them in America probably contains two, if not three, racial heritages; and the average African American today is estimated to be approximately 20 percent white.[28] The dilemma this poses for reparations brings us to the third question concerning litigation.

Who has standing to sue whom? There are, in other words, many African Americans who may want to become plaintiffs against the descendants of the slave owners who owned their ancestors, may file suit only to discover that they themselves are descendants of those same slave owners. If the defendants are identified as the class of people descended from the slave-owning family, the plaintiffs will be in the uncomfortable position of being members of both classes. And this inheritance, in turn, gives an entirely new spin on how we define "collective" guilt.

These are not, in the end, merely academic objections. "The tort model undercuts the moral basis for redress," warns Roy L. Brooks, "and, hence, dishonors the memory of the slaves."[29] This point is an important one to ponder if what is desired are reparations and not merely rage. What, after all, are reparations a recompense *for?* Surprisingly, the answer to this question may be less obvious than it seems, since the answer at first glance seems to be, *for slavery.* But the literature of the reparations movement, including Ta-Nehisi Coates's article, has been understandably reluctant to limit reparations only to the evil fruits of black slavery. The "debt" Randall Robinson described in *The Debt: What America Owes to Blacks* is not owed by America simply for slavery, but includes the entire black experience in America. "Blacks have, and do still" suffer from "slavery and the century of legalized American racial hostility that followed it." By broadening the kinds of damages reparations are intended to repair, Coates and Robinson keep the class of the damaged *large;* but in so doing, the idea of reparations declines from compensation to psychological therapy.

Curiously, Dartmouth College economist Bruce Sacerdote calculated in 2002 that "by comparing outcomes for former slaves and their children and grandchildren to outcomes for free blacks (pre-1865) and their children and grandchildren," the net negative impact imposed by slavery on enslaved African Americans was erased in comparison with free blacks within two generations of emancipation. Sacerdote did not dispute that slavery "had a long-term deleterious effect" on African Americans; but the longest-term effects were on "the stability of the black family," not its economic potential, and involved "loose cohabitation, marriage at too young an age, and family dissolution." In terms, however, of literacy, schooling, and occupation, "descendants of slaves 'caught-up' to the descendants of free blacks within two generations." In other words, the pains and penalties Robinson and Coates complain of have not been attributable to *slavery* since the 1920s. They are instead due to post-slavery racism (in the form of Jim Crow and segregation). Blacks in post–Civil War Tennessee doubled their percentage of landowning between 1870 and 1880; but they were also three times more likely to lose title to their land in the same decade (something which also suggests that even if "forty acres and a mule" had been dispensed to every head of household among the freedpeople, it might not have made a lasting difference). And so the question comes back: for *what,* exactly are we to pay reparations? Given Sacerdote's data, Jim Crow would make a more likely starting place than slavery. But that would sharply diminish the size of the class of individuals involved and deprives the idea of reparations of the emotive power that the historical memory of slavery and its evils has for Americans.[30]

It is one of the strangest omissions in the reparations literature, that in the volume of articles, papers, and books available on this subject, not a single one I have read has ever referred to the event which made the end of slavery possible at all. To read this literature without knowing the history behind it is almost to think that slavery ended by evaporation. We know, of course, that it did not. The American Civil War cost at least 700,000 dead—the equivalent by proportion in today's population, of twenty million casualties, half of them Union soldiers fighting against slavery, and a serious portion of that, African American—not to mention the wounded, maimed, crippled, widowed, and orphaned; it cost $6.6 billion to wage and multiplied the national debt by 400 percent; and it pauperized the South, black and white alike, so much so that the South lagged the other sections of the country in productivity for a century afterward. "Prize your freedom above gold," pleaded Clinton Fisk of the Freedmen's Bureau,

> for it has cost rivers of blood! Go where you will, your eyes will behold great battle-fields, and the graves of brave men, who fell in the mighty struggle which made you free. During the bloody gigantic contest, there has been mourning in tens of thousands of homes, in the North and in the South, and millions now mourn the loss of those they will never see again on earth.[31]

Is this simply a highly elaborated condescension, asking black people to assume humble postures of thanksgiving to white people? Or an example of what Robert Penn Warren sneered at as white Northerners' "treasury of merit"? Only if we believe categorically that the war was fought for tariffs, states' rights, or Union-mending, rather than slavery. And there was no shortage of racists in the South after the war who claimed (and continue to claim) that their Confederacy *was* about states' rights and the economic rivalries of the sections. But Abraham Lincoln knew otherwise, and he charged both North and South with knowing it, too. Slavery "constituted a peculiar

A group of slave children brought to New York City and photographed by Myron H. Kimball in 1863, to demonstrate how thoroughly miscegenation had blurred racial lines in slavery and undermined notions of racial separatism. The photograph was taken as part of a publicity campaign to raise funds for schools for former slaves. The black man at the left, Wilson Chinn, had been branded on the forehead by his owner, Volsey B. Marmillion; Kimball retouched the photograph to emphasize the branding. This photograph also appeared as a lithograph in *Harper's Weekly,* January 30, 1864.

Metropolitan Museum of Art

and powerful interest" in the South, Lincoln said in 1865, and "all knew that this interest was, somehow, the cause of the war." Lincoln often protested that if he could have bought his way around the war by purchasing all the slaves and setting them free, he would cheerfully have done so. In that case, it would have cost the federal government $2.7 billion to emancipate all of the South's slaves—worked out over thirty years, the bill to be rid of slavery would have come to $7.25 a year for every American. But Southern racism only wanted to learn the hard way, and so the price which was paid to end slavery was calculated not in money, but in money *and* blood—the Civil War saddled each American with $75.00 worth of national debt (up from $2.00 in 1860), while the population of Southern white males between the ages of 17 and 45 was cut down by almost 27 percent.[32] The war, Lincoln said, was God's instrument for the ultimate reparation—every drop of blood drawn with the lash had been paid for with blood drawn by the sword.

The fable that the Civil War had nothing to do with slavery used to be a racist staple. And African Americans, in the years after the war, spent enormous effort trying to remind the nation that *they* were the reason the war was fought and that *they* had played a role themselves in winning that war. But it is difficult to follow a divine judgment and a payment in blood with a subsequent demand for payment in money. And so it is now much more common to hear Dorothy Lewis (of the National Coalition of Blacks for Reparations in America, or N'COBRA) or Lerone Bennett argue that white Northerners in the Civil War were only fighting for the Union and not against slavery—as if their deaths did not count in the balances that finally tipped against slavery. Roy L. Brooks, likewise, argues that "ending slavery itself cannot be viewed as a redress for slavery," only as a "precondition for atonement."[33] Except, of course, that slavery did not merely *end;* it was destroyed by force and at enormous cost by the same government and the ancestors of the same people who are now asked to pay reparations.

This is not to say that the bloodshed of the Civil War somehow reads the case for reparations out of court on its own. But it is also a reminder that the case for reparations cannot ignore the cost of the Civil War, either. Not for nothing did Lincoln say that God had judged the United States through "this terrible war as the woe due to those by whom the offense came ... until all the wealth piled up by the bondsman's two hundred and fifty years of unrequited toil shall be sunk." I know that it will be said that the Civil War is irrelevant, that it was waged to preserve the Union and not for black freedom, that the full bill for that "unrequited toil" has not yet been paid, and that Abraham Lincoln was a racist. That gives comfort to some of us who I suspect value rage over rec-

"Incidents of the War: A Burial Party, Cold Harbor, Va.," by John Reekie and Alexander Gardner, highlights an ironic reciprocity, with former slaves hired to rebury the remains of white Union soldiers killed at the Battle of Cold Harbor (June 1864).

New York Public Library

onciliation; the problem is that a people can only live on truth, not rage.

Wendy Kaminer has put her finger on what she calls "an ideological paradox at the heart of demands for reparations." On the one hand, reparations are held up as a gesture of retroactive justice, righting the wrongs that were done to our great-grandparents and before. Yet, there is a deep instinct in the American national psyche which bucks at the notion of defining the present by the definitions of the past. "It allows the past to define our entitlements in the present," Kaminer remarked, "it relies on a belief in the justice of inheritance."[34] If it is racial justice we seek, the greater wisdom lies in addressing it directly, for this generation.

Even as Lincoln appealed to natural law and natural rights, both Romantic particularism and the final elimination of all notions of design in nature were pushing concepts of a universal participation in right and a law out of life, leaving us with struggle and reparation as the only map left to steer by. We have long since jettisoned natural law as what Jeremy Bentham called "simple nonsense: natural and imprescriptible rights, rhetorical nonsense,—nonsense upon stilts," and recast justice (as John Rawls did) as "the fair terms of social cooperation are conceived as agreed by those engaged in it, that is, by free and equal citizens who are born into the society in which they lead their lives." But is this not, in effect, to return us to position of Stephen A. Douglas's "popular sovereignty" instead and to substitute will and power as our Pole stars? Perhaps, in a world come of age, this is all we can expect. But there is a third way, which we must consider next.[35]

3

LINCOLN'S GOD AND EMANCIPATION

It HAS become easy to speak of W. E. B. Du Bois as an elitist. Because he was, and gloried in it. He accumulated degrees, books, and honors like trophies. And it was Du Bois who, in 1903, said frankly that "the Negro race, like all races, is going to be saved by its exceptional men . . . the Talented Tenth; it is the problem of developing the Best of this race that they may guide the Mass away from the contamination and death of the Worst, in their own and other races." He rejoiced at the prospect of a graduating class of Fisk University in 1898, "trained in the liberal arts and subjects in that vast kingdom of culture," who would guide black America's path through "bigotry and falsehood and sin." They would explicate the essence of the black soul and provide the exceptional thinkers who would form a new and instinctive kind of leadership (which, given its parallels to Woodrow Wilson's concept of "the leader," was very much in the overall

Progressive and Romantic modes). This "elitism"—if we may call it that—was what we know pried Du Bois apart from Frederick Douglass, whose interests were in political goals rather than cultural self-discovery, and from Booker T. Washington, who put his faith in the economic leverage to be gained by an entrepreneurial nine-tenths, pursuing the "industrial idea." Washington had no objection to a black man going to "Harvard or Yale and graduate," but he saw "no need why every colored man who graduates at college should go to teaching or preaching" when they could "lay hold of the business and industrial openings in the South during the next 10 years."[1]

The irony of the long, spiraling path of race history in America is that, in the end, neither Du Bois nor Washington was right. The great deliverance of the Second Reconstruction, half a century after Du Bois and Washington parted company, came from an entirely different quarter which neither man had paid much attention to, and that was the black church. Du Bois was unrelenting in his criticism of, and alienation from, churches. "Of course, it is the Churches which are the most discriminatory of all institutions," he exclaimed in 1941, and he dismissed the leadership of the black church as "pretentious, ill-trained men and in far too many cases . . . dishonest and otherwise immoral." They "fall far below expectations," being little more than "hustling businessmen, eloquent talkers, suave companions and hale fellows." The agony of disappointment around Du Bois's broad brow led him in the 1930s to begin a discovery of Marxism which gradually allowed him to blend the Talented Tenth with a Leninist vanguard and arrive at a vision of a racial proletariat, rising to assert itself all over the postcolonial world; mercifully for his own peace of mind, he did not live to see black turn upon black in Rwanda and Uganda, or black upon white in Zimbabwe, or a renascent and militant Islam cast a new Arab slave-shadow across black Africa. And Washington, who was more of an elitist than he liked people to think, was unusually harsh in his criticism of the black church. "A very large number of our colored ministers are morally unfit for their work," he complained in 1890, and he was not a little embarrassed, as an elitist of a different kind, that too many of "our people 'get happy' and 'shout' in church."

> With few exceptions, the preaching of the colored ministry is emotional in the highest degree, and the minister considers himself successful in proportion as he is able to set the

people in all parts of the congregation to groaning, uttering wild screams, and jumping, finally going into a trance. One of the principal ends sought by most of these ministers is their salary, and to this everything else is made subservient. Most of the church service seems to resolve itself into an effort to get money. Not one in twenty has any business standing in the communities where they reside, and those who know them best mistrust them most in matters of finance and general morality.

He had been impressed as a younger man at Wayland Seminary with how students for the ministry seemed to have "more money, were better dressed, wore the latest style of all manner of clothing, and in some cases were more brilliant mentally"—but all the same, "knew more about Latin and Greek when they left school, but . . . less about life and its conditions as they would meet it at their homes." After all, Washington added, "a race but a few years out of slavery . . . had not had time or opportunity to produce a competent ministry."[2]

Yet, it was neither a great scholar nor a well-endowed industrialist who carried the torch for the civil rights movement, but the pastor of the Dexter

Avenue Baptist Church. And Martin Luther King Jr. followed a tradition which stretched all the way back to the abolitionists—white and black. The day that William Lloyd Garrison burnt a copy of the Constitution at the annual Massachusetts Anti-Slavery Society picnic in Framingham was the day Moncure Conway "distinctly recognized that the antislavery cause was a religion" and "that Garrison was a successor of the inspired axe-bearers,—John the Baptist, Luther, Wesley, George Fox." In 1852, William Goodell described intellectual groundwork of the antislavery movement as a religious, Protestant, and evangelical one:

> There were moral, religious, and social influences at work, preparatory to an unprecedented agitation of the slave question. The missionary enterprise, in its youthful vigor, was . . . enlivened with glowing descriptions of the approaching millennium, when all should know the Lord, from the least to the greatest, and sit under their own vines and fig-trees, secure in their rights. . . . Our American love of liberty, equality, and "free institutions" was gratified with the assurance that all the despotisms of the earth were to crumble at the Prince Emanuel's approach! . . .

Whatever our missionary and evangelizing orators intended, whatever they were thinking of, they were God's instruments for putting into the minds of others "thoughts that burned," for the emancipation of the enslaved. . . . The same period was distinguished by "revivals of religion," in which prominence was given to the old doctrine of [Samuel] Hopkins and [Jonathan] Edwards, demanding "immediate and unconditional repentance" of all sin, as the only condition of forgiveness and salvation. This was urged in direct opposition to the vague idea of a gradual amendment, admitting "a more convenient season"—a prospective, dilatory, indefinite breaking off from transgression—an idea that had been settling upon the churches for thirty or forty years previous,—an incubus upon every righteous cause, and every holy endeavor. It is easy to see the bearing of such religious awakenings upon the mode of treating the practice of slaveholding.

And even if Ella Baker was more than a little brutal in her assessment that "the movement made Martin rather than Martin making the movement," the very fact that he was there at all in the front rank, along with Fred Shuttlesworth, Joseph Lowry, Charles K. Steele, and Ralph Abernathy, quoting theologians rather than theorists from his cell in the Birmingham jail, would have come as a surprise to both "Booker T. and W. E. B.," if not to "Frederick D."[3]

Not, I suspect, to Abraham Lincoln, and especially not in the middle of 1862, although it might not have seemed that way at first sight. Lincoln is one of only two American presidents never to have joined a church (the other being Thomas Jefferson), and while other presidents have sat somewhat lightly by their professed memberships, there are few who take lightly the points that church membership confers. Lincoln did, and quite deliberately. We have no record that Lincoln was ever baptized, much less participated in any other churchly or sacramental rites. "I am not much of a judge of religion," Lincoln remarked in 1864, although his upbringing was, curiously, pointed in almost the opposite direction because both his father and stepmother were members of a small, hyper-Calvinistic Baptist sect, and "when 15 years of age or in the year 1824," he "could hear a Sermon—Speech or remark and repeat it accurately. He would go home from the church say to the boys & girls that he could repeat the Sermon—got on Stumps—logs—fences and do it." Then, as his stepsister recalled, "Abe would take down the bible, read a verse—give out a hymn—and we would sing—were good singers. . . . He would preach & we would do the Crying." Even in later life, Lincoln could demonstrate an impressive memory for the Bible. In 1846, a minister, passing by one of Lincoln's political meetings, gave Lincoln a little good-natured heckling "and remarked that *Where the great ones are there will the people be.* Mr. Lincoln replied Ho! Parson, a little more Scriptural: *Where the carcass is, there will the eagles be gathered together!*" [Matthew 24:28] In 1864, when an insurgent dump-Lincoln movement within the Republican party organized an independent convention in Chapin Hall in Cleveland to nominate John Charles Fremont as president, newspaper reports of the convention estimated an attendance of about four hundred delegates. (There were actually 156, according to the *New York Times,* but that would spoil the story.) Lincoln reached unerringly for the text in 1 Samuel 22:2 (KJV) which he thought best described Fremont's rump convention: "And every one that was in distress, and every one that was in debt, and every one that was discontented, gathered themselves unto him; and he became a captain over them: and there were with him about four hundred men."[4]

Knowing the Bible, however, is one thing; believing it another. Nathaniel Grigsby, whose brother married Lincoln's sister while the Lincolns lived in Indiana, explained to William H. Herndon that "I cannot tell you what his notions of the Bible were. He was a great talker on the scriptures and read it a great deal, and

Lincoln delivering his Second Inaugural Address, March 4, 1865, photograph by Alexander Gardner. Facing him, a separate, companion image captures the crowd listening to Lincoln, including for the first time at a presidential inauguration, units of African American soldiers (probably from the Forty-Fifth U.S. Colored Troops).

Library of Congress

he talked about religion as other persons did, but I do not know his view on religion [because] he never made any profession while in Indiana that I know of." Orville Hickman Browning, one of Lincoln's closest political friends, recalled that, during the White House years, Lincoln frequently spent Sunday afternoons in the White House library, reading the Bible; but, added Browning (himself a devout Presbyterian and Bible-reader), he "never knew of [Lincoln] engaging in any other act of devotion. He did not invoke a blessing at table, nor did he have family prayers. What private religious devotions may have been customary with him I do not know. I have no knowledge of any." Even the Lincoln children's babysitter in the White House, Julia Taft Bayne, remarked that Lincoln "read the Bible quite as much for its literary style as he did for its religious or spiritual content. He read it in the relaxed, almost lazy attitude of a man enjoying a good book."[5]

People who heard Lincoln take his oath of office on the same Bible Barack Obama would use at his own swearing-in 144 years later might have been troubled to learn that the twenty-something Lincoln "used to talk Infidelity in the Clerk's office [in Springfield] about the years 1837–40" and "ridiculed the Bible & New Testament." His first law partner, John Todd

Stuart, was alarmed to hear Lincoln hold forth on "the inherent defects, so-called, of the Bible" and deny "that Jesus was the son of God as understood and maintained by the Christian world." Lincoln's unbelief was known broadly enough that in 1847, when he ran for Congress, he was forced to issue a public disclaimer, admitting that though "I am not a member of any Christian Church," he was nevertheless *not* "an open scoffer at Christianity." Maybe not an *open* scoffer, but certainly a private one: one irritated Springfield Presbyterian minister wrote that Lincoln usually spent Sunday mornings at "the railroad shop and . . . the sabbath in reading Newspapers, and telling stories to the workmen."[6]

And yet, Lincoln's unbelief was more in the nature of a reaction than a conviction; he might have the natural-born debater's pleasure at rocking the boats of the pious, but he spoke of his own lack of religion with regret rather than boasting. He was sufficiently alienated from his father, Thomas, that when the old man lay dying in 1851, Lincoln refused a summons to his father's bedside; but he did not mock the consolation that his father's religion held out. "Tell him," Lincoln wrote to his stepbrother, that "our great, and good, and merciful Maker . . . will not turn away from him in any extremity. He notes the fall of a sparrow, and numbers the hairs of our heads; and He will not forget the dying man, who puts his trust in Him." When Parthena Hill, the wife of one of Lincoln's business associates in New Salem, accosted him and asked, "Do you really believe there isn't any future state?" Lincoln's reply was almost regretful: "Mrs. Hill, I'm afraid there isn't. It isn't a pleasant thing to think that when we die that is the last of us." In mid-life Lincoln was even willing to speak of himself as a sort of religious seeker—a seeker who had not yet found, and was not convinced he would find, anything. "Probably it is to be my lot to go on in a twilight, feeling and reasoning my way through life, as questioning, doubting Thomas did," he told Aminda Rogers Rankin, "But in my poor maimed, withered way, I bear with me, as I go on, a seeking spirit of desire for a faith that was with him of the olden time, who, in his need, as I in mine, exclaimed: 'Help thou my unbelief.'" Lincoln might not subscribe to "Church Creeds," said Leonard Swett (another strict Presbyterian layman among Lincoln's friends), but he certainly believed in the existence of natural law and natural rights, "in the great laws of truth, the rigid discharge of duty, his accountability to God, the ultimate triumph of right, and the overthrow of wrong."[7]

Appealing to these "great laws of truth" became an important piece of Lincoln's opposition to slavery because slavery was otherwise legitimated by appeals made by slaveholders to property rights, to theories of racial inferiority, even to parts of the Bible itself. He could speak of himself as "naturally anti-slavery" in 1864, not just because the premises of antislavery seemed to him so self-evident, but because those premises existed mostly in natural law. Slavery was, very simply, "a gross outrage on the law of nature," and *that* explained why a loathing for slavery amounted to human instinct: "Have not all civilized nations, our own among them, made the Slave trade capital, and classed it with piracy and murder?" Lincoln demanded, "Is it not held to be the great wrong of the world?"[8]

It did not surprise Lincoln, then, that slavery's defenders retaliated by denying the existence of any such natural right to liberty, or denied that it applied to black people, or denied that natural law had more authority than raw majority rule. In the hands of proslavery radicals like John C. Calhoun of South Carolina, Jefferson and the Declaration were a colossal mistake. "All men are not created equal," Calhoun announced. "Instead, then, of all men having the same right to liberty and equality," liberty and equality are merely social conventions to be handed out as "high prizes" to certain races "in their most perfect state." Lincoln's old nemesis, Stephen A. Douglas, affirmed that democracy is morally autonomous. It "leaves the people to do just as they please, and to shape their institutions according to what they may conceive to be their interests both for the present and the future." Any state or territory in the Union whose voters wanted a "slave-State constitution" must have "a right to it. It is none of my business which way the slavery clause is decided. I care not whether it is voted down or voted up."[9]

Lincoln thought this was not only absurd, but dangerous. Mere majority rule cannot reverse natural law, natural rights, or natural institutions. Natural law embodied what Wendell Phillips called "that absolute essence of things which lives in the sight of the Eternal and Infinite; not as men judge it in the rotten morals of the nineteenth century, among a herd of States that calls itself an empire, because it raises cotton and sells slaves." In fact, Lincoln believed, it was the underlying substructure of natural rights which ensured that the "empire" Phillips disparaged would not go entirely off the rails and spin into some self-destructive abyss. Trying to override the natural rights to life, liberty, and the pursuit of happiness of other people purely by majority will would leave *you* unprotected when the majority turned its unrestricted powers on *you*. "Our defense is in the preservation of the spirit which prizes liberty as the heritage of all men, in all lands, everywhere," and not just as some local statute which can be sent up or sent down by the next referendum. Lincoln warned,

> Destroy this spirit and you have planted the
> seeds of despotism around your own doors.
> Familiarize yourselves with the chains of
> bondage, and you are preparing your own
> limbs to wear them. Accustomed to trample on
> the rights of those around you, you have lost
> the genius of your own independence, and
> become the fit subjects of the first cunning
> tyrant who rises.[10]

Like many a secular-minded optimist in the middle of the nineteenth century, Lincoln had a sublime confidence in the power of progress. Isaac Cogdal, who had known Lincoln as far back as his youthful days in New Salem, remarked that "the great substantial groundworks of Religion" in Lincoln were his confidence "in the progress of man and of nations." He had once described slavery as the one "retrograde in-stitution in America" precisely because it stuck out so incongruously from the confident progress of the world toward more and greater freedom, "under-mining the principles of progress, and fatally vio-lating the noblest political system the world ever saw."

But progress is precisely what the first eighteen months of the Civil War offered no evidence of: slavery, which ought to have been headed for the dustbin of history, had shown itself resourceful in wooing sympathy from Britain and France, and even small-scale Prussia's "Iron Chancellor," Otto von Bis-marck, warned Carl Schurz years later that there "was something in me that made me instinctively sympathize with the slaveholders, as the aristocratic party, in your Civil War." Worst of all, the Rebel armies had been victorious on one battlefield after another, and his own principal general, George B. Mc-Clellan was not only an ineffective battlefield com-mander, but a political dissenter who had told Lin-coln in July that any move on the president's part in the direction of emancipation would "rapidly disin-tegrate our present Armies"—as though McClellan had neither power nor responsibility to prevent that. One mark of how badly the war had shaken Lincoln's confidence in progress emerged in a peculiar question he asked Orville Hickman Browning: "Browning, suppose God is against us in our view on the subject in this country, and our method of dealing with it?" It was the first time that the devout Browning could recall that Lincoln showed any hint "that he was thinking deeply of what a higher power than man sought to bring about by the great events then transpiring." And perhaps about even more than what "a higher power" or a natural law was yet to bring about.[11]

By September 1862, the main Rebel army, Robert E. Lee's Army of Northern Virginia, had actually gone on the offensive, crossed the Potomac River, and was poised to invade Pennsylvania. Lincoln, as was his habit, began trying to understand the dilemma of progress gone awry on paper, and what he came up with was a series of private notes which sounded like a combination of theology and geometry. "The will of God prevails," he wrote, as though he was stating an axiom. (And surely, if God really *is* God, his will *must* prevail, or else he would not be God.) In this war, both sides claim "to act in accordance with the will of God." But neither has exactly achieved what would surely be the result—victory—which having the will of God on their side would produce. After all, God, "by his mere quiet power, on the minds of the now contestants . . . could have either saved or destroyed the Union without a human contest." But he had not only evidently willed that war should begin, but (because it was moving in such unpredictable directions) that it should "proceed in a direction that neither side had anticipated." That, for Lincoln, was proof enough that God's "purpose is something different from the purpose of either party," something new that neither side had planned. And the unavoidable conclusion he had to draw from that was that the unplanned-for result must be the emancipation of the slaves.[12]

But for Lincoln to speak in these terms was not only to talk about God—any worldly-wise politician can do that—but about a God who was not merely a remote force or a faceless universal power, but a personal, intelligent, and willing God who intervened in the affairs of this world to direct them in ways that they could not even begin to imagine. Three weeks later, after Lee's army had been brought to battle at Antietam and driven back across the Potomac, Lincoln gave this realization an even sharper point when he laid before his Cabinet the text of an Emancipation Proclamation, which by virtue of his war powers as commander-in-chief, would free every slave in Rebel hands. Once the Rebel army invaded Maryland, he explained to his assembled cabinet secretaries on September 22, 1862, "I determined, as soon as it should be driven out of Maryland, to issue a Proclamation of Emancipation." And he had done so on the strength of a "promise" he had "made to myself, and—(hesitating a little)—to my Maker. The rebel army is now driven out, and I am going to fulfil that promise."[13]

To these hard-bitten political veterans, nothing could have been more utterly bizarre than to listen to a president announce that he was about to make the most important policy decision of his administration—and perhaps American history—on the strength of conversations with a voice out of the whirlwind. This statement, coming from a man of so minimal a religious profile as Lincoln, jolted even the most religious of those cabinet secretaries, Salmon P. Chase, "who was sitting near him," into asking Lincoln to repeat himself, as though Chase could not believe what he was hearing as a sober statement of policy: "He asked the President if he correctly understood him. Mr. Lincoln replied: I made a solemn vow before God, that if General Lee was driven back from Pennsylvania, I would crown the result by the declaration of freedom to the slaves." This might not be the reasoning employed under most political circumstances, but "he had promised his God that he would do it," and there it was: "He had made a vow, a covenant, that if God gave us the victory in the approaching battle, he would consider it an indication of Divine will, and that it was his duty to move forward in the cause of emancipation." It might, he admitted, with a staggering understatement, "be thought strange . . . that he had in this way submitted the disposal of matters when the way was not clear to his mind what he should do." But Lincoln had concluded that "God had decided this question in favor of the slaves. He was satisfied it was right" and "was confirmed and strengthened in his action by the vow and the results." When the final version of the proclamation was signed for implementation on January 1, 1863, Lincoln included in its otherwise spare and legal wording the closing—and legally useless—flourish that emancipation was "an act of justice" on which he invoked "the considerate judgment of mankind, and the gracious favor of Almighty God." *Legally* useless, perhaps, but useful for pointing out a justice which might exist beyond the strict tenets of constitutional law.[14]

None of these statements turned Lincoln into a true believer, much as many true believers then and now have wanted to seize upon the emancipation moment and other moments like it to proclaim Lincoln a convert to Christianity, or Swedenborgianism, or Spelling Reform, or a hundred other persuasions, political as well as religious which treat converts as trophies more than saints. But it does mark a peculiar passage in the life of this man that he felt pressed to reach back into the long-closed cellar of his ancestral faith, to a God who speaks and acts, rather than merely a force whose power is so conveniently remote that he can be picked up and played with at our whim. *Have you got good religion?* we want to ask him, and hear the reply *Certainly, Lord.* That did not mean that God was less of a mystery to Lincoln than before—simply that God was now a *personal* mystery. Over the remaining two-and-a-quarter years of his life, Lincoln would return time and again to visit this mystery, until in 1865, he believed that he had found some measure of understanding why slavery had come and why the great war had been necessary to make it go. "American Slavery," he said, is an offence; of that, he had no doubt. But we would be wrong to imagine that it was only the slaveholder's offense; all Americans—North and South alike—stood in some measure guilty of tolerating it, apologizing for it, turning the gaze away from it, practicing it, funding it, benefiting from it—and that, he believed, was the

reason why the end of slavery required a war so terrible. A crime so terrible, and so widely shared, demanded an expiation which assumed the same di-
mensions as the crime itself. If that is the case—and
he always couched this idea tentatively, prefaced by
if, so that he would not be thought to have a view-
port into God better than others'—and God "gives
to both North and South, this terrible war, as the
woe due to those by whom the offence came," should
we be surprised at the costs it exacts? "Shall we dis-
cern therein any departure from those divine attributes which the believers in a Living God always
ascribe to Him?" In the face of a guilt in which all
had sinned and fallen short of the glory of God, the
only appropriate behavior for victors and van-
quished alike was to conduct themselves with humility and repentance,

> With malice toward none; with charity for all;
> with firmness in the right, as God gives us to see
> the right, let us strive on to finish the work we
> are in; to bind up the nation's wounds; to care
> for him who shall have borne the battle, and for
> his widow, and his orphan—to do all which may
> achieve and cherish a just, and a lasting peace,
> among ourselves, and with all nations.

All were under the judgment of God—not just under the obligations of natural law, but under God.[15]

The farther we move in time from emancipation, the less remarkable it seems and the easier it is to take for granted, so that the actual mechanisms of Lincoln's proclamation—its numerous exemptions (including the slaves in the border states), its use of "military necessity" as a justification, its disenchanted and legalistic language, the long delay between the outbreak of war and the proclamation itself—seem inexplicable, and sometimes conveniently so. We are more inclined today to discount the purity of Lincoln's motives, to wonder with accusing intent why he did not free *all* the slaves, or free them earlier, to diminish his agency by appealing to the pressures brought to bear on him by others of nobler spirit—the abolitionists, the fugitive slaves and "contrabands," the Radical Republicans in Congress. In the neo-Confederate mind, this inclination reinforces the urge to allow nothing of the white Confederacy to be owed to slavery; in the neo-abolitionist mind, it reinforces a parallel urge to allow nothing to be owed to Lincoln. For in a world come of age, we *self*-emancipate, we bridle at codependency, we will do for ourselves what needs to be done. It repudiates not only Lincoln, but the Union, and the Union dead, and in the long run, the all-controlling Providence that hung in the background of Lincoln's mental geography.

Self-emancipation, as a thesis, actually has a long history, stretching back to Herbert Aptheker and Du Bois in the 1930s and the notion of the Civil War as a "general strike" of the slaves, and popularized more recently by Vincent Harding and Barbara J. Fields. In fact, it has even longer roots as a concept, beginning with Marx's "Critique of the Gotha Program" ("the emancipation of the working class must be the act of the working class itself") and Marx's warning against the snares of cooperative alliances of workers with "vulgar socialism." In the context of slave emancipation in the United States, self-emancipation has the additional attraction of promoting black agency, in just the style Du Bois would have appreciated. In one recent example, it is not Lincoln who emancipated anyone, but self-emancipated slaves who forced Lincoln to formulate policies that reflected the self-emancipated reality. Slaves "were not waiting for Lincoln. They would start the war themselves" rather than "simply waiting for either the Lord or the Yankees to give them freedom," until "by 1863, there was a full-blown inner civil war going on within the South."[16]

But there were no "pressures" on Lincoln to emancipate anyone—the abolitionists were never a political constituency large enough to be worth factoring with; and we have no idea what numbers of fugitives or "contrabands" fled into Union lines, although what *is* certain is that they exercised no political clout in the white North, much less on its president. For self-emancipated slaves to have "pushed the nation toward legal emancipation," they would have had to constitute at least a critical political mass; but even if we grant William Henry Seward's offhand estimate at Hampton Roads in 1865 that 200,000 slaves had found refuge with the Union armies, we are still talking about less than 5 percent of the total enslaved population of the Confederate states. If anything, the presence of such "contrabands" on Northern soil actually generated serious racist reaction in the North, so any pressure the "contrabands" were exerting was just as liable to move in the opposite direction from emancipation. Far from amounting to a Nat Turner-style "inner civil war" in the South, what impressed Northern onlookers was that "there has not been a single slave insurrection of any magnitude"—although this lack of a slave uprising was held as proof, not of slave compliance with slavery, but as a rebuke to "the wicked authors of this Rebellion."[17]

But there is also a legal problem lurking behind the self-emancipation thesis, which can be called "the Shawshank Illusion." ("Shawshank," in this example, refers to the 1994 movie *The Shawshank Redemption,* where the closing scene shows Morgan Freeman, who has jumped the terms of his probation, striding happily toward his prison-inmate friend, Tim Robbins, who had escaped from jail in one of the more sensational versions of the cinematic jailbreak.) The characters at the end of *The Shawshank Redemption* are apparently gloriously and happily free on the beach at Zihuatanejo. In fact, they are not, whatever the illusion conjured up by the movie. They are simply fugitives, and they can be arrested, extradited, and reimprisoned at will, and cannot own property and enjoy civil standing in their own names. Fugitive slaves were, likewise, free only de facto; that escape did not confer de jure freedom. In law, they remained fugitives, and would have done so till the end of their days without Lincoln's proclamation. And if the Civil War had ended in some form of negotiated settlement (after the election of George McClellan, for instance), it is difficult to believe that Southern negotiators would not have demanded rendition of their fugitives (that suggestion was, in fact, made to Lincoln in August 1864), and equally difficult to believe that war-weary Northern whites would not have colluded in such rendition if that would bring peace. What was needed was a de jure declaration of freedom (of the nature of the *Somerset* ruling, which declared slavery a legal impossibility in England in 1770), legally terminating the slaves' status as chattels, and that could come from no other quarter but Abraham Lincoln. Sickening as it is to realize, self-emancipation by war in 1865 would probably not have offered much more protection in the federal courts than did Dred Scott's earlier plea of self-emancipation by relocation in 1857. Anyone who imagines that, if the Civil War had ended with anything less than a total Union military victory, Southerners would not have bargained and negotiated for the return of those fugitives (as they did after the Revolution and the War of 1812), must certainly have a higher opinion of the pliability of slaveholders than I do. (Kevin Willmott's "mock-umentary" *C.S.A.* is a useful, even if extravagant, reminder of how easily slavery might have been repristinated around the world if the Civil War had had any other ending than the one Lincoln forced upon it.)[18]

Let us not, at the same time, fall off the other side of our horse and lapse into the notion that the slaves did *nothing*. Nothing underscored the enthusiasm with which the slaves greeted even the rumor of emancipation more than the demonstrations of welcome offered to Union troops, not to mention the numerous covert and subversive aids they offered to the Union armies. "Those who had hitherto regarded the relation of master and slave as one of mutual affection," warned the surgeon of the Seventy-seventh New York, "had only to witness these unique demonstrations of rejoicing at our approach, and the seemingly certain destruction of the slave owners, to be convinced that the happiness and contentment claimed for those in servitude was but a worthless fiction."

> Great numbers of negroes flocked to the
> roadside, to welcome the Union army.... All
> hoped that we would shortly overtake and
> destroy the rebel army, their masters included....
> Gathering in crowds along the way side, [they]
> would grasp the hands of the Union soldiers,
> calling down all manner of blessing upon them,
> and leaping and dancing in their frantic delight.
> One gray-haired old patriarch ... exclaimed, in a

loud voice, "bress de Lord! I'se been praying for yous all to come all dis time; and now I'se glad yous got so far; and I pray de Lord dat yous may keep on, and conquer def and hell and de grave!"

Union officers discovered that "negroes are our only friends" in the South, and General Ormsby Mitchell cited "two instances" in which "I owe my own safety to their faithfulness." It did not take long for Union soldiers to realize that "if I want to find out anything hereabouts, I hunt up a Negro." Willard Glazier, an officer in the Second New York Cavalry and a prisoner

Slaves concealing and protecting the escaped Union prisoner-of-war Willard Glazier, from Glazier's *The Capture, The Prison-Pen and the Escape* (New York: U.S. Publishing, 1868).

of war, escaped his captors in South Carolina in 1864 and also found that "these people, so patient under oppression ... were ever faithful and devoted to those whom they believed to be the friends of their race ... and the cruelties practised upon them seem rather to have opened their hearts to sympathy than to have hardened them into vindictiveness." Glazier was moved by night by slaves, floated in a boat repaired by slaves for him, and finally made his way to Union lines in northern Georgia on December 23, 1864, in the company of a free black guide, March Dasher.

Even William T. Sherman, who was as close to being a white supremacist as a prominent Union general could be, relied on the informal network of African American informants for intelligence on Confederate movements. The arrival of Union troops in the vicinity of a plantation would trigger desertions en masse "and everything like subordination and restraint was at an end." Once the recruitment of black soldiers began in 1863, Lincoln reminded a mass meeting in his hometown of Springfield that "commanders of our armies in the field who have given us our most important successes, believe the emancipation policy, and the use of colored troops, constitute the heaviest blow yet dealt to the rebel-

lion; and that at least one of those important successes, could not have been achieved when it was,
but for the aid of black soldiers." By the end of his
life, even the ferocious Sherman was willing to admit
that "equality of citizenship and personal freedom
of action" must be the basis of the nation. "Let us
freely accord to the Negro his fair share of influence
and power, trusting the perpetuity of our institutions to the everlasting principles of human nature
which tolerate all races and all colors, leaving each
human being to seek in his own sphere 'the enjoy-
ment of life, liberty and happiness.'"[19]

That Lincoln chose to use "military necessity,"
rather than an appeal to "justice," as his rationale for
emancipation is sometimes pled as a last-ditch defense against Lincoln the Emancipator, as though
emancipation was merely a trick to induce African
American cooperation in the war. But it bears remembering that presidents are not elected to do justice, but
to execute the laws, and that any presidential proclamation which went unclothed in the constitutional
armor of "military necessity," or which failed to recog-
nize that "military necessity," had no application to
border states where no war had ever existed, was begging to be destroyed in a federal court system whose
head was, at that moment, the same chief justice

who had authored *Dred Scott v. Sanford*. If anything, all the pressures Lincoln felt—from the courts, the generals, even his cabinet secretaries—pushed in the opposite direction, promising injunctions, lost elections, and perhaps a military coup. Those who "are devoutly praying that President Lincoln may have faith to move mountains" were reminded by Lois Bryan Adams of "the little hills that beset and block up his way to the mountains" or of "the miserable dripping, drizzling rains that pelt and blind and chill him every step he takes!"[20] That is the backdrop which our overfamiliarity with the *fact* of emancipation causes us to miss. That none of these dire results actually occurred does not mean that they could not have happened, or that Lincoln was not obliged to reckon with them; if anything, it means that his strategy in emancipation was wiser than the serpent's, even as it now appears to have been as harmless as the dove's.

No one, in the end, was less ashamed to admit dependence than Lincoln. "I attempt no compliment to my own sagacity," he said in 1864. "At the end of three years struggle the nation's condition is not what either party, or any man devised, or expected. God alone can claim it."[21] This statement is often dismissed by the Lincoln-haters on the political Right as a cynical attempt by Lincoln to off-load his responsibility for triggering the war in the first place; but it utterly baffles the political Left, which prefers to substitute for Lincoln's *God* some mysterious force of growth, or sympathy, or simply political canniness, all of which have as their single common denominator the wish to find a respectable ground upon which Lincoln can be seen acting independently. For in a world come of age, a world which has become conscious of itself and grown self-confident to the point where we may all get along perfectly well in all questions of importance without fathers and mothers, without communities, without people whom we do not like or do not wish to acknowledge, we balk at the notion that we owe anything to others, or that we should become as little children. "Thy Godlike crime," wrote Byron (about Prometheus, but it might easily have been written for Lincoln), "was to be kind,

> To render with thy precepts less
> The sum of human wretchedness,
> And strengthen Man with his own mind."

This humiliates us; this reminds us of what we owe others and owe our past; this denies us agency, and keeps us from autonomy. We do not merely discover Lincoln the half-heart, or Lincoln the racist; we actually *prefer* him, for the freedom it gives to *us*. But humility is the handmaid of justice, and especially justice which must come in the company of war. "Our nation is being tried by fire and blood," wrote Edward Bullard in 1863, "because nothing else would produce a state of humility and justice in our minds."[22]

However, I am not confident that in a world come of age, skepticism about the adulthood of the world would be any more successful than an attempt to put a grown-up back into a child's skin, to make someone dependent on things or people or concepts which they are no longer dependent upon, or to thrust them into problems which are no longer felt to be problems any more. But I do believe that we only live when we live for others, and in acknowledgment of others. And I suspect that Wendell Phillips was right when he asserted that the death of the master-slave relationship would arrive with "a mixed race, to whom, in its virtues, belongs in the future a country."[23] Only when we find ways in which we can live with each other in the innocence and lack of shame that is so manifest in children that the world which has come of age can avoid drowning in its own maturity of organization, greed, and hedonism. *For of such is the kingdom of Heaven.*

NOTES

Preface

1. John McKnight, *The Careless Society: Community and Its Counterfeits* (New York: Basic Books, 1995), xix, 22–24, 106, 179.

2. Alexis de Tocqueville, *Democracy in America,* ed. Harvey Mansfield and Delba Winthrop (Chicago: University of Chicago Press, 2000), 513–514; William Julius Wilson, *The Bridge over the Racial Divide: Rising Inequality and Coalition Politics* (Berkeley: University of California Press, 1999), 77.

1. The Unwanting of Abraham Lincoln

1. Abraham Lincoln, "Temperance Address," February 22, 1842, in *Collected Works of Abraham Lincoln,* ed. Roy P. Basler et al. (New Brunswick, NJ: Rutgers University Press, 1953), 1:279.

2. George Boutwell, in *Reminiscences of Abraham Lincoln by Distinguished Men of His Time,* ed. Allen Thorndike Rice (New York: North American,

1886), 107, 133; "Abraham Lincoln" [eulogy at Lowell, Massachusetts, April 19, 1865], in *Speeches and Papers Relating to the Rebellion* (Boston: Little, Brown, 1867), 362.

3. Edward F. Bullard, *The Nation's Trial: The Proclamation; Dormant Powers of the Government; The Constitution a Charter of Freedom, and Not "a Covenant with Hell"* (New York: C. B. Richardson, 1863), 2–33; Henry Greenleaf Pearson, *The Life of John A. Andrew, Governor of Massachusetts, 1861–1865* (Boston: Houghton, Mifflin, 1904), 2:50–51; Moncure Daniel Conway, *Autobiography, Memories and Experiences* (Boston: Houghton, Mifflin, 1904), 1:345; *Fifty Years in Camp and Field: Diary of Major-General Ethan Allan Hitchcock, U.S.A.*, ed. W. A. Crofut (New York: G. P. Putnam, 1909), 444; Charles D. Drake, "The Proclamation of Emancipation" [January 28, 1863], in *Union and Anti-Slavery Speeches, Delivered during the Rebellion* (1864; repr., New York: Greenwood Press, 1969), 202; Hannibal Hamlin to Abraham Lincoln, September 25, 1862, in Charles Eugene Hamlin, *The Life and Times of Hannibal Hamlin* (Cambridge, MA: Riverside Press, 1899), 439.

4. Dietrich Bonhoeffer to Eberhard Bethge, June 8, 1944, in *Letters and Papers from Prison: The Enlarged Edition,* ed. Eberhard Bethge (New York: Macmillan, 1972), 325–327; and Dietrich Bonhoeffer,

Ethics, ed. Eberhard Bethge (New York: Macmillan, 1965), 358.

5. William Henry Herndon to Jesse W. Weik, February 16, 1887, in *The Hidden Lincoln, from the Letters and Papers of William H. Herndon* (New York: Viking Press, 1938), 175.

6. George Ward Nichols, *The Story of the Great March from the Diary of a Staff Officer* (New York: Harper, 1865), 59; A. M. French, *Slavery in South Carolina and the Ex-Slaves; or, The Port Royal Mission* (New York: W. M. French, 1862), 136, 138; Jacqueline Jones, *A Dreadful Deceit: The Myth of Race from the Colonial Era to Obama's America* (New York: Basic Books, 2013), 168; John Dennett, "The South as It Is: From Our Special Correspondent; XVI," October 20, 1865, *Nation* 1 (November 2, 1865): 559; Anne Sarah Rubin, *Through the Heart of Dixie: Sherman's March and American Memory* (Chapel Hill: University of North Carolina Press, 2014), 80.

7. "Washington News Sent North," *Washington National Intelligencer,* June 4, 1863; William F. Grant to Thomas Grant, Newport News, VA, July 21, 1862, Gilder-Lehrman Collection, New-York Historical Society; "A Colored Man," September 1863, in *Freedom's Soldiers: The Black Military Experience in the Civil War,* ed. Ira Berlin et al. (Cambridge: Cambridge University Press, 1998), 110; Clarence Mohr, *On the Threshold of Freedom: Masters and Slaves in*

Civil War Georgia (Athens: University of Georgia Press, 1985), 288–289; Charles A. Page, *Letters of a War Correspondent,* ed. J. R. Gilmore (Boston: L. C. Page, 1899), 337–338.

8. Frederick Douglass, "The Inaugural Address," April 1861, "The President and His Speeches," September 1862, and "The United States Cannot Remain Half-Slave and Half-Free, Speech on the Occasion of the Twenty-First Anniversary of Emancipation in the District of Columbia," April 16, 1883, in *Frederick Douglass: Selected Speeches and Writings,* ed. Philip Foner (Chicago: Lawrence Hill Books, 1999), 433, 435, 511–512, 667; John Eaton, *Grant, Lincoln and the Freedmen: Reminiscences of the Civil War* (New York: Longmans, Green, 1907), 175.

9. *Slavery in the Clover Bottoms: John McCline's Narrative of His Life during Slavery and the Civil War,* ed. Jan Furman (Knoxville: University of Tennessee Press, 1998), 30; Sam Mitchell and Sam Polite, in *The American Slave, A Composite Autobiography,* vol. 3, pt. 3, *South Carolina Narratives,* ed. George P. Rawick (Westport, CT: Greenwood Press, 1972), 203, 275; William H. Wiggins, *O Freedom! Afro-American Emancipation Celebrations* (Knoxville: University of Tennessee Press, 1987), 71; Charity Austin, in *North Carolina Slave Narratives: A Folk History of Slavery in North Carolina from Interviews with Former Slaves*

(Bedford, MA: Applewood Books, 2006), 59–60; Rubin, *Through the Heart of Dixie,* 71.

10. French, *Slavery in South Carolina and the Ex-Slaves,*143; Edwin E. Marvin, *The Fifth Regiment Connecticut Volunteers: A History* (Hartford, CT: Wiley Waterman & Eaton, 1889), 238; Thomas John Chew Williams, *History of Frederick County, Maryland* (1910; repr., Baltimore: Regional, 1967), 1:848; William Henry Singleton, *Recollections of My Slavery Days,* ed. K. M. Charron and D. S. Cecelski (Raleigh: North Carolina Division of Archives and History, 1999), 49; Benjamin Quarles, *Lincoln and the Negro* (New York: Oxford University Press, 1962), 182, 233; "Hall of Congress, Richmond, April 6, 1865," in *Thomas Morris Chester, Black Civil War Correspondent: His Dispatches from the Virginia Front,* ed. R. J. M. Blackett (Baton Rouge: Louisiana State University Press, 1989), 294–297.

11. Carolyn L. Harrell, *When the Bells Tolled for Lincoln: Southern Reaction to the Assassination* (Macon, GA: Mercer University Press, 1997), 57–58; Jacob Thomas, in *"No Sorrow Like Our Sorrow": Northern Protestant Ministers and the Assassination of Abraham Lincoln,* ed. David B. Chesebrough (Kent, OH: Kent State University Press, 1994), 4; "Richmond, April 30, 1865," in *Thomas Morris Chester, Black Civil War Correspondent,* 329; Henry Highland Garnet, *Celebration by the Colored People's Educational*

*Monument Association in Memory of Abraham Lincoln
on the Fourth of July 1865 in the Presidential Grounds*
(Washington: McGill & Witherow, 1865), 14; Elijah
Marrs, *Life and History of the Rev. Elijah P. Marrs*
(Louisville, KY: Bradley & Gilbert, 1885), 22;
Alexander Heritage Newton, *Out of the Briars: An
Autobiography and Sketch of the Twenty-Ninth Regiment
Connecticut Volunteers* (1910; repr., Miami: Mnemo-
syne, 1969), 65.

12. William Sanders Scarborough, "The Party of
Freedom and the Freedmen—A Reciprocal Duty,"
February 11, 1899, and Alexander Walters,
"Abraham Lincoln and Fifty Years of Freedom,"
February 12, 1909, in *Masterpieces of Negro Eloquence:
The Best Speeches Delivered by the Negro from the
Days of Slavery to the Present Time,* by Alice Moore
Dunbar-Nelson (New York: Bookery, 1914), 221, 329;
William H. Wiggins, *O Freedom! Afro-American
Emancipation Celebrations* (Knoxville: University of
Tennessee Press, 1987), 90; Albert E. Pillsbury,
Lincoln and Slavery (Boston: Houghton Mifflin,
1913), 92.

13. Newton, *Out of the Briars,* 76; J. G. Nind, in *Soldiers'
Letters: From Camp, Battle-field and Prison,* ed. Lydia
Minturn Post (New York: Bunce Huntington,
1865), 291; John W. Forney, *Anecdotes of Public Men*
(New York: Harper & Bros., 1873), 1:321–322.

14. Randall Kennedy, *The Persistence of the Color Line: Racial Politics and the Obama Presidency* (New York: Pantheon, 2011), 9.

15. "Abolition of Slavery Forever Impossible," *Old Guard* 3 (April 1865): 178.

16. Lois Bryan Adams, *Letter from Washington, 1863–1865,* ed. Evelyn Leasher (Detroit, MI: Wayne State University Press, 1999), 93, 171, 232–233.

17. Phillips Brooks, *Our Mercies of Re-Occupation: A Thanksgiving Sermon Preached at the Church of the Holy Trinity, Philadelphia, November 26, 1863* (Philadelphia: William S. & Alfred Martien, 1863), 22–23; Theodore Tilton, "One Blood of All Nations," February 27, 1864, and "The First and the Second Revolution," November 29, 1866, in *Sanctum Sanctorum; or, Proof-Sheets from an Editor's Table* (New York: Sheldon, 1870), 104–105, 135–136; Joel Prentiss Bishop, *Thoughts for the Times* (Boston: Little, Brown, 1863), 34–35; William Lloyd Garrison, in Greg Carter, *The United States of United Races: A Utopian History of Racial Mixing* (New York: New York University Press, 2013), 47; "White Supremacy and Negro Subordination," *Old Guard* 5 (May 1865): 193.

18. Thaddeus Stevens, "Remarks on Black Soldiers, April 30, 1864, in Congress," and "Speech on Conquered Provinces, April 4, 1863, to the Union League of Lancaster," in *The Selected Papers of*

Thaddeus Stevens, ed. B. W. Palmer (Pittsburgh: University of Pittsburgh Press, 1997), 1:392, 457; Charles Sumner to Mary Peabody Mann, June 27, 1864, in *The Selected Letters of Charles Sumner,* ed. B. W. Palmer (Boston: Northeastern University Press, 1990), 2:247, 270; George Julian, *Political Recollections, 1840 to 1872* (1884; repr., New York: Negro Universities Press, 1970), 251; George A. Levesque, "Boston's Black Brahmin: Dr. John S. Rock," *Civil War History* 26 (December 1980), 335-336; Adams, *Letter from Washington,* 33; David Blight, *Frederick Douglass' Civil War: Keeping Faith in Jubilee* (Baton Rouge: Louisiana State University Press, 1989), 186; Lawrence S. Berry, in Michael W. Fitzgerald, *Urban Emancipation: Popular Politics in Reconstruction Mobile, 1860–1890* (Baton Rouge: Louisiana State University Press, 2002), 126; Frederick Douglass, in Waldo E. Martin, *The Mind of Frederick Douglass* (Chapel Hill: University of North Carolina Press, 1984), 222.

19. J. M. Sturtevant, "The Destiny of the African Race in the United States," *Continental Monthly* 2 (May 1863): 602; Stevens, "To Simon Stevens," September 5, 1862, and "The Government of the Rebellious States," May 2, 1864, in *Selected Papers,* 1:323, 470; Ivan Hannaford, *Race: The History of An Idea in the West* (Baltimore, MD: Johns Hopkins University press, 1996), 17, 246, 278; Karl Christoph Vogt,

Lectures on Man: His Place in Creation, and in the History of the Earth, ed. James Hunt (Longman, Green, Longman and Roberts, 1864), 172, 192; James Hunt, *Introductory Address on the Study of Anthropology* (London: Trubner, 1863), 3–4; Christine Bolt, *Victorian Attitudes to Race* (London: Routledge & Kegan Paul, 1971), 18; "Is Race an Accident," *Walla Walla Statesman,* August 3, 1866; *The American Slave, a Composite Autobiography,* vol. 2, pt. 1, *South Carolina Narratives,* 5–6.

20. David W. Blight, *Race and Reunion: The Civil War in American Memory* (Cambridge, MA: Harvard University Press, 2001), 138–139.

21. Julian, *Political Recollections,* 243; Hans L. Trefousse, *Andrew Johnson: A Biography* (New York: W. W. Norton, 1989), 183; Howard B. Means, *The Avenger Takes His Place: Andrew Johnson and the 45 Days That Changed the Nation* (Orlando, FL: Harcourt, 2006), 55; Hans L. Trefousse, "Andrew Johnson and the Freedmen's Bureau," in *The Freedmen's Bureau and Reconstruction: Reconsiderations,* ed. Paul A. Cimbala and Randall M. Miller (New York: Fordham University Press, 1999), 42; "Fortress Monroe, Jan. 20, 1866," in the *Freed-Man,* May 1, 1866, 249; W. M. Grosvenor, "The Rights of the Nation and the Duty of Congress," *New Englander and Yale Review* 24 (October 1865): 756; Oliver Otis Howard, in John & LaWanda Cox, "General O. O. Howard

and the 'Misrepresented Bureau,'" *Journal of Southern History* 19 (November 1953): 440; Col. J. W. Shaffer to Trumbull, December 25, 1865, in Horace White, *The Life of Lyman Trumbull* (New York: Houghton Mifflin, 1913), 242.

22. Christopher Memminger to Carl Schurz, April 26, 1871, in *Speeches, Correspondence and Political Papers of Carl Schurz,* ed. Frederic Bancroft (New York: G. P. Putnam's, 1912), 2:256; Glenna Schroeder-Lein and Richard Zuczek, eds., *Andrew Johnson: A Biographical Companion* (Santa Barbara, CA: ABC-CLIO, 2001), 7; diary entry for May 25, 1865, in *The Private Journal of Henry William Ravenal, 1859–1887,* ed. A. R. Childs (Columbia: University of South Carolina Press, 1947), 238.

23. George Boutwell, "The Usurpation," *Atlantic Monthly* 18 (October 1866): 506; Frederick Douglass, "Reconstruction," *Atlantic Monthly* 18 (December 1866): 764; Grosvenor, "The Rights of the Nation and the Duty of Congress," 756.

24. Harry V. Jaffa, *Equality and Liberty: Theory and Practice in American Politics* (New York: Oxford University Press, 1965), 153–154; Jonathan W. White, *Emancipation, the Union Army and the Re-Election of Abraham Lincoln* (Baton Rouge: Louisiana State University Press, 2014), 4, 9, 35; Barrington Moore, *Social Origins of Dictatorship and Democracy: Lord and Peasant in the Making of the Modern World* (London:

Penguin, 1967), 130; Clement Laird Vallandigham, "How Shall the Union Be Preserved," February 20, 1861, in *The Record of Hon. C. L. Vallandigham on Abolition: The Union, and the Civil War* (Columbus, OH: J. Walter, 1863), 72; Samuel Osgood, "Our Lessons in Statesmanship," *Harper's Monthly* 30 (March 1865): 477.

25. "Radicalism," *Washington Democrat,* March 11, 1865; Larry A. Greene, "The Emancipation Proclamation in New Jersey and the Paranoid Style," *New Jersey History* 91 (Summer 1973): 121; William Seraile, *New York's Black Regiments during the Civil War* (New York: Routledge, 2001), 102; David Montgomery, *Beyond Equality: Labor and the Radical Republicans, 1862–1872* (New York: Knopf, 1967), 52, 57–58; Scott L. Malcolmson, *One Drop of Blood: The American Misadventure of Race* (New York: Farrar, Straus & Giroux, 2000), 350; Mia Bay, *The White Image in the Black Mind: African-American Ideas about White People, 1830–1925* (New York: Oxford University Press, 2000), 90.

26. Michael Les Benedict, "A New Look at the Impeachment of Andrew Johnson," *Political Science Quarterly* 113 (Fall 1998): 493–511; Mark Wahlgren Summers, *A Dangerous Stir: Fear, Paranoia, and the Making of Reconstruction* (Chapel Hill: University of North Carolina Press, 2009), 146–147; Mark Wahlgren Summers, *The Ordeal of the Reunion: A*

New History of Reconstruction (Chapel Hill: University of North Carolina Press, 2014), 357, 365, 368.

27. Stephen C. Neff, *Justice in Blue and Gray: A Legal History of the Civil War* (Cambridge: Harvard University Press, 2010), 148–149; Archibald Cox, *The Court and the Constitution* (Boston: Houghton Mifflin, 1987), 111; Jonathan W. White, "The Strangely Insignificant Role of the U.S. Supreme Court during the Civil War," *Journal of the Civil War Era* 3 (June 2013): 211–238; Michael A. Ross, "Justice Miller's Reconstruction: The Slaughter-House Cases, Health Codes, and Civil Rights in New Orleans, 1861–1873," *Journal of Southern History* 64 (November 1998): 652; Orestes Brownson, "Third Annual Message of President Lincoln to both Houses of Congress," *Brownson's Quarterly Review* 1 (January 1864): 94; "Wendell Phillips at Cooper Institute," *New York Times,* December 23, 1863.

28. Frederick Douglass, "The Supreme Court Decision," October 22, 1883, in *Frederick Douglass: Selected Speeches and Writings,* 686.

29. Joseph Foster Lovering, *Services for the Use of the Grand Army of the Republic* (Boston: Headquarters of the Grand Army of the Republic, 1881), 14; Barbara Gannon, *The Won Cause: Black and White Comradeship in the Grand Army of the Republic* (Chapel Hill: University of North Carolina, 2011), 25–26.

30. Jeremy Atack and Peter Passell, *A New Economic View of American History,* 2nd ed. (New York: W. W. Norton, 1994), 476–477; *The Preservation of the Union An Economic Necessity* (New York: W. C. Bryant, 1863), 5–6; Henry Ward Beecher, "Liberty Under Laws," December 28, 1862, in *Patriotic Addresses in America and England, from 1850 to 1885, on Slavery, the Civil War, and the Development of Civil Liberty in the United States,* ed. J. R. Howard (Boston: Pilgrim Press, 1887), 405–406; James L. Huston, *Calculating the Value of the Union: Slavery, Property Rights, and the Economic Origins of the Civil War* (Chapel Hill: University of North Carolina Press, 2003), 234–235; Abraham Lincoln, "Speech at Kalamazoo, Michigan," August 27, 1856, in *Collected Works,* 2:364; Robert Dale Owen, *The Wrong of Slavery, the Right of Emancipation and the Future of the African Race in the United States* (Philadelphia: J. P. Lippincott, 1864), 116–117.

31. Wendell Phillips, "The State of the Country," January 21 and May 11, 1863, in *Speeches, Lectures, and Letters* (Boston: James Redpath, 1863), 544; John Greenleaf Whittier, "Snow-Bound," in *American Poetry: The Nineteenth Century,* vol. 1: *Freneau to Whitman* (New York: Library of America, 1993), 488–489; Paul David Phillips, "Education of Blacks in Tennessee during Reconstruction,

1865–1870," *Tennessee Historical Quarterly* 2 (Summer 1987): 99–100.

32. "Land for the Landless," *Nation* 4 (May 16, 1867): 395; Carl Shurz, *The Reminiscences of Carl Schurz* (London: John Murray, 1909), 3:161.

33. Alex Lichtenstein, "Was the Emancipated Slave a Proletarian?" *Reviews in American History* 26 (March 1998): 139; Alex Lichtenstein, "Proletarians or Peasants? Sharecroppers and the Politics of Protest in the Rural South, 1880–1940," *Plantation Society in the Americas* 5 (Fall 1998), 311–312; Larian Angelo, "Wage Labour Deferred: The Recreation of Unfree Society in the US South," *Journal of Peasant Studies* 22 (July 1995): 584; Heather Cox Richardson, *The Greatest Nation of the Earth: Republican Economic Policies during the Civil War* (Cambridge: Harvard University Press, 1997), 180; Heather Cox Richardson, *Westward from Appomattox: The Reconstruction of America after the Civil War* (New Haven, CT: Yale University Press, 2007), 150–153; Whitelaw Reid, *After the War: A Southern Tour: May 1, 1865, to May 1, 1866* (London: Sampson Low, Son & Marston, 1866), 59, 64; Hans L. Trefousse, *The Radical Republicans: Lincoln's Vanguard for Racial Justice* (New York: Knopf, 1968), 373; B. Moore, *Social Origins of Dictatorship and Democracy*, 142; K. Stephen Prince, *Stories of the South: Race and the Reconstruction of Southern Identity, 1865–1915* (Chapel

Hill: University of North Carolina Press, 2014), 20–27; Steven Hahn, "Class and State in Postemancipation Societies: Southern Planters in Comparative Perspective," *American Historical Review* 95 (February 1990): 86, 94–95.

34. Daniel W. Stowell, *Rebuiding Zion: The Religious Reconstruction of the South, 1863–1877* (New York: Oxford University Press, 1998), 47–48, 80; Erik Arneson, *Waterfront Workers of New Orleans: Race, Class, and Politics, 1863–1923* (New York: Oxford University Press, 1991), 26; Steven Hahn, *A Nation under Our Feet: Black Political Struggles in the Rural South, from Slavery to the Great Migration* (Cambridge, MA: Harvard University Press, 2003), 304–305; Victoria E. Bynum, *The Long Shadow of the Civil War: Southern Dissent and Its Legacies* (Chapel Hill: University of North Carolina Press, 2010), 35, 99.

35. John Hope Franklin and Loren Schweninger, *Runaway Slaves: Rebels on the Plantation* (New York: Oxford University Press, 1999), 214; William Wells Brown, *Clotelle; or, The Colored Heroine* (1867; repr., Miami: Mnemosyne, 1969), 21; Edward Holland, *A Refutation of the Calumnies Circulated against the Southern and Western States, Respecting the Institution and Existence of Slavery among Them* (Charleston, SC: A. R. Miller, 1822), 35–36; Allen C. Guelzo, *Lincoln's Emancipation Proclamation: The End of*

Slavery in America (New York: Simon & Schuster, 2004), 78.

36. Justin A. Nystrom, *New Orleans after the Civil War: Race, Politics, and a New Birth of Freedom* (Baltimore: Johns Hopkins University Press, 2010), 103–104, 131; David C. Rankin, "The Origins of Black Leadership in New Orleans during Reconstruction," *Journal of Southern History* 40 (August 1974): 426–427; Peter Kolchin, *First Freedom: The Responses of Alabama's Blacks to Emancipation and Reconstruction* (Westport, CT: Greenwood Press, 1972), 140–141; Jones, *Dreadful Deceit,* 177–178; Bay, *White Image in the Black Mind,* 66.

37. Julius Lester, *Look Out, Whitey! Black Power's Gon' Get Your Mama!* (New York: Dial Press, 1968), 37.

2. *The Antislavery World of Abraham Lincoln*

1. H. Ford Douglass, in James M. McPherson, *The Negro's Civil War: How American Negroes Felt and Acted during the War for the Union* (New York: Pantheon, 1965), 7; Wendell Phillips, "Lincoln's Election," November 7, 1860, in *Speeches, Lectures, and Letters* (Boston: James Redpath, 1863), 302; William Lloyd Garrison to Oliver Johnson, October 7, 1861, in *Letters of William Lloyd Garrison: Let the Oppressed Go Free, 1861–1867,* ed. Walter M. Merrill (Cambridge, MA: Harvard University Press, 1979), 5:37; Edward Bates to Wyndham

Robertson, November 3, 1860, in Marvin R. Cain, *Lincoln's Attorney General: Edward Bates of Missouri* (Columbia: University of Missouri Press, 1965), 119.

2. W. E. B. Du Bois, "The Problem of Problems," in *W. E. B. DuBois Speaks: Speeches and Addresses, 1890–1919,* ed. Philip S. Foner (New York: Pathfinder Press, 1970), 261; W. E. B. Du Bois, "Abraham Lincoln," *Crisis,* May 1922, and "Again Lincoln," *Crisis,* September 1922, in *W. E. B. DuBois: Writings,* ed. Nathan Huggins (New York: Library of America, 1986), 1196, 1197–1198; W. E. B. Du Bois, "The Negro and Social Reconstruction," 1936, in *Against Racism: Unpublished Essays, Papers, Addresses, 1887–1961,* ed. Herbert Aptheker (Amherst: University of Massachusetts Press, 1985), 146; Mitch Kachun, "Celebrating Freedom: Juneteenth and the Emancipation Festival Tradition," in *Remixing the Civil War: Meditations on the Sesquicentennial,* ed. Thomas J. Brown (Baltimore: Johns Hopkins University Press, 2011), 75–76; "An Open Letter Sent to Howard President James M. Nabrit," February 1968, in *The Eyes on the Prize Civil Rights Reader: Documents, Speeches, and Firsthand Accounts from the Black Freedom Struggle,* ed. Clayborne Carson et al. (New York: Viking Penguin, 1991), 462–463.

3. Joseph Gillespie to William H. Herndon, January 31, 1866, in *Herndon's Informants: Letters, Interviews and Statements about Abraham Lincoln,* ed.

Rodney O. Davis and Douglas L. Wilson (Urbana: University of Illinois Press, 1998), 183–184; George Julian, *Political Recollections, 1840 to 1872* (1884; repr., New York: Negro Universities Press, 1970), 183; Salmon Chase to A. Sankey Latty, December 8, 1860, in A. Sankey Latty Papers, Manuscript Division, Library of Congress, Washington, DC; Isaac Newton Arnold, *The History of Abraham Lincoln and the Overthrow of Slavery* (Chicago: Clarke, 1866), 300, 685–686; "Garrison on Lincoln: A Speech Delivered Soon after the Latter's Death," *New York Times,* November 11, 1881; William Lloyd Garrison to Helen E. Garrison, June 9 and 11, 1864, in *Letters of William Lloyd Garrison,* 5:210, 212.

4. Abraham Lincoln, "Protest in the Illinois Legislature on Slavery," March 3, 1837, "Speech at Peoria, Illinois," October 16, 1854, "Speech at Springfield," July 27, 1858, "First Debate with Stephen A. Douglas at Ottawa Illinois," August 21, 1858, "Speech at Carlinville," August 31, 1858, "Fourth Debate with Stephen A. Douglas at Charleston, Illinois," September 18, 1858, and "To Albert G. Hodges," April 4, 1864, in *Collected Works of Abraham Lincoln,* ed. Roy P. Basler et al. (New Brunswick, NJ: Rutgers University Press, 1953), 1:75, 2:255, 519–520, 3:16, 79, 145, 7:281. See Brian Lamb's interview of Lerone Bennett, in *800 Non-Fiction*

Authors in Hour-Long Interviews, April 1989–December 2004, BookNotes, September 10, 2000, www.book notes.org/Watch/158187-1/Lerone+Bennett.aspx; Lerone Bennett, *Forced into Glory: Abraham Lincoln's White Dream* (Chicago: Johnson, 1999), 40.

5. John McWhorter, "Why Juneteenth's Not My Thing," *Root,* June 19, 2008.

6. Abraham Lincoln, "Speech at Springfield, Illinois," June 26, 1857, in *Collected Works,* 2:404, 406; Kurt Vonnegut Jr., "Harrison Bergeron" (1961), in *Welcome to the Monkey House* (1968; repr., New York: Dial Press, 2010), 7–14.

7. Abraham Lincoln, "Fragment on Government," July 1, 1854, and "Speech at Chicago, Illinois," July 10, 1858, in *Collected Works,* 2: 221, 499–500.

8. Lincoln, "Speech at Springfield, Illinois," October 4, 1854, and "Speech at Peoria, Illinois," October 16, 1854, in *Collected Works,* 2:245, 265.

9. Abraham Lincoln, "Fragment on Slavery," July 1, 1854, "To George Robertson," August 15, 1855, "Speech at Kalamazoo, Michigan," August 27, 1856, "Speech at Cincinnati, Ohio," September 17, 1859, "Speech at New Haven, Connecticut," March 6, 1860, in *Collected Works,* 2:222, 318, 364, 3:459, 4:24; Gabor Boritt, *Lincoln and the Economics of the American Dream* (Memphis, TN: Memphis State University Press, 1978), 281.

10. Abraham Lincoln, "Address Before the Young Men's Lyceum of Springfield, Illinois," January 27, 1838, and "To Joshua F. Speed," August 24, 1855, in *Collected Works*, 1:110, 2:320; Henry Bromwell, in *Recollected Words of Abraham Lincoln*, ed. Don Fehrenbacher and Virginia Fehrenbacher (Stanford, CA: Stanford University Press, 1996), 40; Robert V. Bruce, "The Riddle of Death," in *The Lincoln Enigma: The Changing Faces of an American Icon* (New York: Oxford University Press, 2001), 130–145.

11. "Abraham Lincoln," *North American Review* 100 (January 1865): 8, 11; Gillespie to Herndon, January 31, 1866, in Davis and Wilson, *Herndon's Informants*, 183–184; Lincoln, "Speech at Peoria, Illinois," October 16, 1854, "Seventh and Last Debate with Stephen A. Douglas at Alton, Illinois," October 15, 1858, and "Speech at New Haven, Connecticut," March 6, 1860, in *Collected Works*, 2:268, 276, 3:312, 4:16; James M. Ashley, *Success of the Calhoun Revolution: The Constitution Changed and Slavery Nationalized by the Usurpations the Supreme Court* (Washington, DC: Buell & Blanchard, 1860), 27.

12. W. H. Herndon to Gillespie, February 20, 1866, Joseph Gillespie Papers, Chicago Historical Society; Abraham Lincoln, "Temperance Address," February 22, 1842, in *Collected Works*, 1:279; W. H. Herndon, January 15, 1874 and November 24, 1882,

and W. H. Herndon to C. O. Poole, January 5, 1886, and "Lincoln the Individual," in *The Hidden Lincoln, from the Letters and Papers of William H. Herndon,* ed. Emmanuel Hertz (New York: Viking, 1938), 83, 89, 121, 415.

13. Abraham Lincoln, "Speech at Worcester, Massachusetts," September 12, 1848, and "Address on Colonization to a Deputation of Negroes," August 14, 1862, in *Collected Works,* 2:3, 5:372–373; Leonard Swett to W. H. Herndon, January 17, 1866, in Davis and Wilson, *Herndon's Informants,* 162.

14. Lincoln, "Speech at Chicago, Illinois," July 10, 1858, "Speech at Carlinville, Illinois," August 31, 1858, and "Speech at Cincinnati, Ohio, September 17, 1859, in *Collected Works,* 2:501, 3:79, 80, 446; "Interview between President Lincoln and a Committee of Colored Men," *Washington Evening Star,* August 15, 1862. Skeptical of Lincoln's "critics" like Lerone Bennett and George Frederickson, Edward E. Baptist describes Lincoln's comments on race as "cagey qualifications" which allowed him to dodge "race-baiting" while sticking to his fundamental opposition to slavery. See Edward E. Baptist, *The Half Has Never Been Told: Slavery and the Making of American Capitalism* (New York: Basic Books, 2014), 382–383.

15. George Park Fisher, "Of the Distinction between Natural and Political Rights," *New Englander and*

Yale Review 23 (January 1864): 21, 25–26; Abraham Lincoln, "Last Public Address," April 11, 1865, in *Collected Works*, 8:403; Robert E. May, *Slavery, Race, and Conquest in the Tropics: Lincoln, Douglas, and the Future of Latin America* (Cambridge University Press, 2013), 251; John Rhodehamel and Louise Taper, *Right or Wrong, God Judge Me: The Writings of John Wilkes Booth* (Urbana: University of Illinois Press, 1997), 15.

16. Thomas Holt, *The Problem of Race in the Twenty-First Century* (Cambridge, MA: Harvard University Press, 2000), 121; Mark Ellis, *Race, Harmony and Black Progress: Jack Woofter and the Interracial Cooperation Movement* (Bloomington: Indiana University Press, 2013), 3–13; Jane Dailey, *Before Jim Crow: The Politics of Race in Postemancipation Virginia* (Chapel Hill: University of North Carolina Press, 2000), 6.

17. Ta-Nehisi Coates, "The Case for Reparations," May 21, 2014, www.theatlantic.com/features /archive/2014/05/the-case-for-reparations/361631/; a somewhat more theatrical version of this demand was uttered by rap singer Azealia Banks, upping the ask to $100 trillion because "we are the children of the people who perished in the name of modern capitalism and we deserve a piece of that f**king pie." See "Azealia Banks Calls for

Reparations for Slavery," *The Independent,* December 30, 2014.

18. James M. McPherson, *Ordeal By Fire: The Civil War and Reconstruction* (New York: Knopf, 1982), 548–549; Fisk, in Robert Tracy McKenzie, "Freedmen and the Soil in the Upper South: The Reorganization of Tennessee Agriculture, 1865–1880," *Journal of Southern History* 59 (February 1993): 67; Thaddeus Stevens, "Claims of Loyalists for Damages," in Cong. Globe, 40th Cong., 1st Sess. (1867); Roy E. Finkenbine, "Historians and Reparations," *Organization of American Historians Newsletter* (February 2006): 3; Gavin Wright, *Sharing the Prize: The Economics of the Civil Rights Revolution in the American South* (Cambridge, MA: Harvard University Press, 2013), 35; Ernest Lyon, "Emancipation and Racial Advancement," in *Masterpieces of Negro Eloquence: The Best Speeches Delivered by the Negro from the Days of Slavery to the Present Time,* by Alice Moore Dunbar-Nelson (New York: Bookery, 1914), 465–466; Vincene Verdun, "If the Shoe Fits, Wear It: An Analysis of Reparations to African Americans," *Tulane Law Review* 67 (February 1993): 600–607; Robert L. Allen, "Past Due: The African American Quest for Reparations," *Black Scholar* 28 (Summer 1998), 2–6; Lord Anthony Gifford, "Legal Arguments in Support of

Reparations," unpublished paper presented to the First Pan-African Congress on Reparations, Abuja, Nigeria, April 27-29, 1993, www.swagga.com /arguments.htm; Eleazar Barkan, *The Guilt of Nations: Restitution and Negotiating Historical Injustices* (New York: Norton, 2000), 3, 27; Niall Ferguson, *The Pity of War: Explaining World War I* (New York: Basic Books, 1998), 403, 404.

19. Thomas U. Berger, *War, Guilt and World Politics after World War II* (Cambridge: Cambridge University Press, 2012), 12-29.

20. William H. Kimball, "Our Government and the Blacks," *Continental Monthly* 5 (April 1864): 433-434; George Boutwell, "Treason the Fruit of Slavery," *Speeches and Papers relating to the Rebellion and the Overthrow of Slavery* (Boston: Little, Brown, 1867), 177-178; James Blaine, "The Fourteenth Amendment as a Basis of Reconstruction," *Political Discussions, Legislative, Diplomatic, and Popular, 1856–1886* (Norwich, CT: Henry Bill, 1887), 67.

21. Martha Biondi, "The Rise of the Reparations Movement," *Radical History Review* 87 (Fall 2003): 12-13.

22. Rhonda V. Magee, "The Master's Tools, from the Bottom Up: Responses to African-American Reparations Theory in Mainstream and Outsider Remedies Discourse," *Virginia Law Review* 79 (May 1993), 868; John McWhorter, *Authentically Black:*

Essays for the Silent Majority (New York: Gotham Books, 2003), 2–22; Robert L. Allen, "Past Due," 3.

23. Roy L. Brooks, *Atonement and Forgiveness: A New Model for Black Reparations* (Berkeley: University of California Press, 2004), 141; Saul Levmore, "Changes, Anticipations, and Reparations," *Columbia Law Review* 99 (November 1999): 1690–1699; Jack Hitt, W. E. Gary, Alexander Pires, Richard Scruggs, and Dennis Sweet, "Making the Case for Racial Reparations," *Harper's Magazine* (November 2000): 37, 51.

24. Jeffrey Ghannam, "Repairing the Past," *American Bar Association Journal* (November 2000): 39–43; Conrad Worrill, in Chris Jenkins and Hamil Harris, "Slavery's Children Seek Reparations," *Washington Post,* August 10, 2002, C1, C10; Sweet, "Making the Case for Racial Reparations," 46; Baptist, *The Half Has Never Been Told,* 245–248.

25. Cato v. United States of America, No. 94-17102, 1995 U.S. App. (9th Cir. December 4, 1995); Mathew Manweller, "Can a Reparations Package Be a Bill of Attainder?" *Independent Review* 6 (Spring 2001): 555–571; Robert A. Toombs, "Boston Lecture on Slavery," in *Oratory and Rhetoric in the Nineteenth-Century South: A Rhetoric of Defense,* by W. Stuart Towns (Westport, CT: Praeger, 1998), 65.

26. George Shedler, "Responsibility for the Estimation of the Damages of American Slavery," *University of*

Memphis Law Review 33 (Winter 2003): 341. The assumption that the U.S. government is somehow statutorily culpable for slavery is a common error, made even in the "findings and purpose" section of the Conyers bill. See Allen, "Past Due," 8, and J. Angelo Corlett, *Race, Racism and Reparations* (Ithaca, NY: Cornell University Press, 2003), 194-195, 203-205.

27. Paul Finkelman, *An Imperfect Union: Slavery, Federalism, and Comity* (Chapel Hill: University of North Carolina Press, 1981), 96-97; William H. Freehling, *The Road to Disunion: Secessionists at Bay, 1776–1854* (New York: Oxford University Press), 133.

28. Annette Gordon-Reed, *Thomas Jefferson and Sally Hemings: An American Controversy* (Charlottesville: University Press of Virginia, 1997), 209; Scott Malcolmson, *One Drop of Blood: The American Misadventure of Race* (New York: Farrar, Straus and Giroux, 2001), 106; R. Chakraborty, M. I. Kamboh, M. Nwankwo et al., "Caucasian Genes in American Blacks," *American Journal of Genetics* 50 (1992): 145-155.

29. Brooks, *Atonement and Forgiveness*, 139.

30. Bruce Sacerdote, "Slavery and the Intergenerational Transmission of Human Capital," unpublished paper, National Bureau of Economic Research (NEBR) Summer Institute 2000, Cambridge, MA, 4-5, 25. In fact, even more

sensational, Sacerdote's comparative analysis concludes that "relative to whites born in the same region," postemancipation blacks and Southern whites alike enjoyed a measure of economic convergence. What they converged on was pitifully less than the rest of the United States was enjoying between 1880 and 1920, but Sacerdote at least raises the possibility that regionalism has to take a place beside racism in accounting for the disparate income levels of black and white Americans. Roy L. Brooks's response to Sacerdote suggests that Sacerdote has underestimated the *psychological* harms of slavery; but that only pushes the question of reparations on the uncertain ground of subjective perception, something which litigation (as opposed to legislation) is ill suited to address. See Brooks, *Atonement and Forgiveness,* 45–47; and McKenzie, "Freedmen and the Soil," 79–80.

31. Clinton Fisk, *Plain Counsels for Freedmen: In Sixteen Lectures* (Boston: American Tract Society, 1866), 9.

32. Jeremy Atack and Peter Passell, *A New Economic View of American History,* 2nd ed. (New York: W. W. Norton, 1994), 356, 359–360.

33. Brooks, *Atonement and Forgiveness,* 193–194.

34. Wendy Kaminer, "Up from Reparations," *American Prospect* 11 (May 22, 2000), 38.

35. Jeremy Bentham, "Anarchical Fallacies, Being a Critical Examination of the Declaration of

Rights," (1792) in *The Works of Jeremy Bentham: Now First Collected; under the Superintendence of his Executor, John Bowring* (Edinburgh: William Tait, 1839), 2:501; John Rawls, *Political Liberalism* (New York: Columbia University Press, 1993), 23.

3. Lincoln's God and Emancipation

1. W. E. B. Du Bois, "The Talented Tenth," in *The Negro Problem: A Series of Articles by Representative American Negroes of To-Day* (New York: James Pott, 1903), 33; Mia Bay, " 'The World Was Thinking Wrong about Race': *The Philadelphia Negro* and Nineteenth-Century Science," in *W. E. B. DuBois, Race, and the City:* The Philadelphia Negro *and Its Legacy,* ed. Michael Katz and Thomas Sugrue (Philadelphia: University of Pennsylvania Press, 1998), 52; Adolph L. Reed, *W. E. B. Du Bois and American Political Thought: Fabianism and the Color Line* (New York: Oxford University Press, 1997), 53–54; David Levering Lewis, *W. E. B. Du Bois: A Biography, 1868–1963* (New York: Henry Holt, 2009), 183; Booker T. Washington to T. Thomas Fortune, March 1, 1899, in *The Booker T. Washington Papers, Volume Five, 1899–1900,* ed. L. Harlan & R. Smock (Urbana: University of Illinois Press, 1976), 46; Kwame Anthony Appiah, "Battling with Du Bois," *New York Review of Books* 58 (December 22, 2011): 81, 84–5; Stanley Crouch and Playthell Banjamin,

Reconsidering the Souls of Black Folk (Philadelphia: Running Press, 2002), 175–176.

2. W. E. B. Du Bois, "The Negro Church," in *Du Bois on Religion,* ed. Phil Zuckerman (Lanham, MD: AltaMira Press, 2000), 46; Brian L. Johnson, *W. E. B. Du Bois: Toward Agnosticism, 1868–1934* (Lanham, MD: Rowman & Littlefield, 2008), 129–137; "Religion," in *W. E. B. Du Bois: An Encyclopedia,* ed. Gerald Horne and Mary Young (Westport, CT: Greenwood Press, 2001), 181; Adam Fairclough, *Teaching Equality: Black Schools in the Age of Jim Crow* (Athens: University of Georgia Press, 2001), 13; Booker T. Washington, *The Future of the American Negro* (Boston: Small, Maynard, 1900), 121; Booker T. Washington, "The Colored Ministry: Its Defect and Needs," *Christian Union* 42 (August 14, 1890): 199; Booker T. Washington, *Up from Slavery: An Autobiography* (New York: Doubleday, Page, 1907), 88, 230; Ernest L. Gibson, "The Envy of Erudition: Booker T. Washington and the Desire for a Du Boisian Intellectuality," *Black Scholar* 43 (Spring 2013): 60–61.

3. Robert H. Abzug, *Cosmos Crumbling: American Reform and the Religious Imagination* (New York: Oxford University Press, 1994), 144; Moncure Daniel Conway, *Autobiography, Memories and Experiences* (Boston: Houghton, Mifflin, 1904), 1:184; William Goodell, *Slavery and Anti-slavery: A*

History of the Great Struggle in Both Hemispheres; With a View of the Slavery Question in the United States (New York: William Harned, 1852), 388; Anne C. Loveland, "Evangelicalism and 'Immediate Emancipation' in American Antislavery Thought," *Journal of Southern History* 32 (May 1966): 172; Nick Kotz, *Judgment Days: Lyndon Baines Johnson, Martin Luther King Jr., and the Laws That Changed America* (New York: Houghton Mifflin, 2006), 51.

4. Abraham Lincoln, "Story Written for Noah Brooks," December 3, 1864, in *Collected Works of Abraham Lincoln*, ed. Roy P. Basler et al. (New Brunswick, NJ: Rutgers University Press, 1953), 8:154; Dennis Hanks interview, September 8, 1865, Matilda Johnston Moore interview, September 8, 1865, and Andrew Goodpasture interview, March 31, 1869, in *Herndon's Informants: Letters, Interviews and Statements about Abraham Lincoln,* ed. Rodney O. Davis and Douglas L. Wilson (Urbana: University of Illinois Press, 1998), 104, 109, 573; "The Cleveland Convention," *New York Times,* June 1, 1864; David Herbert Donald, *Lincoln* (New York: Simon and Schuster, 1995), 503.

5. Nathaniel Grigsby to William H. Herndon, January 21, 1866, in *Herndon's Informants,* 169; Orville Hickman Browning, in *An Oral History of Abraham Lincoln: John G. Nicolay's Interviews and Essays,* ed. Michael Burlingame (Carbondale:

Southern Illinois University Press, 1996), 130; Julia Taft Bayne, *Tad Lincoln's Father* (Boston: Little, Brown, 1931), 183–184.

6. James Matheny, interview with William H. Herndon, March 2, 1870, and John Todd Stuart, interview with William H. Herndon, March 2, 1870, in *Herndon's Informants,* 576; Abraham Lincoln, "Handbill Replying to Charges of Infidelity," July 31, 1846, in *Collected Works,* 1:382; G. W. Pendleton, October 1, 1860, in *An Oral History of Abraham Lincoln,* 155.

7. Abraham Lincoln, "To John D. Johnston," January 12, 1851, in *Collected Works,* 2:97; Parthena Hill, in Walter B. Stevens, *A Reporter's Lincoln,* ed. Michael Burlingame (Lincoln: University of Nebraska Press, 1998), 12; Aminda Rogers Rankin, in *Recollected Words of Abraham Lincoln,* ed. Don Fehrenbacher and Virginia Fehrenbacher (Stanford, CA: Stanford University Press, 1996), 373; David Davis, interview with William H. Herndon, September 20, 1866, and Leonard Swett to William H. Herndon, January 17, 1866, in *Herndon's Informants,* 168, 350.

8. Abraham Lincoln, "Speech at Springfield, Illinois," October 4, 1854, in *Collected Works,* 2:245.

9. John C. Calhoun, "Speech on the Oregon Bill," in *Union and Liberty: The Political Philosophy of John C. Calhoun,* ed. R. M. Lence (Indianapolis: Liberty

Fund, 1992), 566, 568–569; Douglas, "Speech in the Senate on the Lecompton Constitution" (March 22, 1857), in Clark E. Carr, *Stephen A. Douglas: His Life, Public Services, Speeches and Patriotism* (Chicago, 1909), 231; Stephen A. Douglas, "The President's Message," in Cong. Globe, 35th Cong., 1st Sess. (1857), 18.

10. Wendell Phillips, "Harper's Ferry," November 1, 1859, in *Speeches, Lectures and Letters* (Boston: James Redpath, 1863), 272–273; Abraham Lincoln, "Speech at Edwardsville, Illinois," September 11, 1858, in *Collected Works*, 3:94.

11. Isaac Cogdal interview, 1865–66, in *Herndon's Informants,* 441; Abraham Lincoln, "Speech at Peoria, Illinois," October 16, 1854, in *Collected Works*, 2:276; Carl Schurz, "Talks with Bismarck," *McClure's Magazine* 31 (August 1908): 367; George B. McClellan, "To Abraham Lincoln," July 7, 1862, in *The Civil War Papers of George B. McClellan: Selected Correspondence, 1860–1865,* ed. Stephen W. Sears (New York: Ticknor & Fields, 1989), 344–345, and in *The War of the Rebellion: A Compilation of the Official Records of the Union and Confederate Armies* (Washington, DC: Government Printing Office, 1881–1906), ser. 1, vol. 11, pt. 1, p. 73; Browning interview with John G. Nicolay, June 17, 1875, in *Oral History of Abraham Lincoln,* 5.

12. Abraham Lincoln, "Meditation on the Divine Will," September 2, 1862, in *Collected Works,* 5:403.

13. Salmon Chase, diary entry for September 22, 1862, in *Inside Lincoln's Cabinet: The Civil War Diaries of Salmon P. Chase,* ed. David Herbert Donald (New York: Longmans, Green, 1954), 150.

14. Gideon Welles, diary entry for September 22, 1862, in *Diary of Gideon Welles, Secretary of the Navy under Lincoln and Johnson,* ed. John T. Morse (Boston: Houghton Mifflin, 1911), 1:143; Francis Bicknell Carpenter, *Six Months at the White House with Abraham Lincoln: The Story of a Picture* (New York: Hurd & Houghton, 1867), 89–90; Abraham Lincoln, "Emancipation Proclamation," January 1, 1863, in *Collected Works,* 6:30.

15. Abraham Lincoln, "Second Inaugural Address," March 4, 1865, in *Collected Works,* 8:332; Dietrich Bonhoeffer, in *Ethics,* ed. Eberhard Bethge (New York: Macmillan, 1965), 310.

16. David Williams, *I Freed Myself: African American Self-Emancipation in the Civil War Era* (New York: Cambridge University Press, 2014), 19, 56, 86; David Roediger, *Seizing Freedom: Slave Emancipation and Liberty for All* (New York: Verso, 2014), 8–11.

17. John Goode, "The Peace Conference in Hampton Roads," *Southern Historical Society Papers* 29 (January–December 1901), 188; Francis Wayland,

"Letter to a Peace Democrat," *Atlantic Monthly* 12 (December 1863): 777.

18. Barrington Moore, *Social Origins of Dictatorship and Democracy: Lord and Peasant in the Making of the Modern World* (London: Penguin, 1967), 153.

19. George T. Stevens, *Three Years in the Sixth Corps* (Albany: S. R. Gray, 1866), 59; William W. Freehling, *The South v. The South: How Anti-Confederate Southerners Shaped the Course of the Civil War* (New York: Oxford University Press, 2001), 102; Willard Glazier, *The Capture, the Prison Pen, and the Escape: Giving a Complete History of Prison Life in the South* (Hartford, CT: H. E. Goodwin, 1867), 287–306; Mitchell to E. M. Stanton, May 4, 1862, in *The War of the Rebellion*, ser. 1, vol. 10, pt. 2, p. 162; Robert O'Connell, *Fierce Patriot: The Tangled Lives of William Tecumseh Sherman* (New York: Random House, 2014), 111–112; Stephen V. Ash, *When the Yankees Came : Conflict and Chaos in the Occupied South, 1861–1865* (Chapel Hill: University of North Carolina Press, 1995), 154–156; Abraham Lincoln, "To James C. Conkling," August 31, 1863, in *Collected Works*, 6:423 (Lincoln was quoting a letter he had received from Ulysses S. Grant in which Grant described emancipation and "arming the negro" as "the heavyest blow yet given the Confederacy"); William T. Sherman, "Old Shady,

with a Moral," *North American Review* 147 (October 1888): 368.

20. Lois Bryan Adams, January 2, 1865, *Letter from Washington, 1863–1865,* ed. Evelyn Leasher (Detroit, MI: Wayne State University Press, 1999), 224.

21. Abraham Lincoln, "To Albert G. Hodges," April 4, 1864, in *Collected Works,* 7:282.

22. Dietrich Bonhoeffer, in *Letters and Papers from Prison: The Enlarged Edition,* ed. Eberhard Bethge (New York: Macmillan, 1972), 325; Mia Bay, *The White Image in the Black Mind: African-American Ideas about White People, 1830–1925* (New York: Oxford University Press, 2000), 200-201, 204, 206; George Gordon Byron, "Prometheus," in *British Poets of the Nineteenth Century,* ed. C. H. Page (Boston: B. H. Sanborn, 1904), 214; Edward F. Bullard, *The Nation's Trial: The Proclamation; Dormant Powers of the Government; The Constitution a Charter of Freedom, and Not "a Covenant with Hell"* (New York: C. B. Richardson, 1863), 233.

23. Wendell Phillips, in Greg Carter, *The United States of United Races: A Utopian History of Racial Mixing* (New York: New York University Press, 2013), 66.

INDEX